A F

A DI

A Private Language?

A Dip into Welsh Literature

Marion Eames

First edition—1997

ISBN 1 85902 468 8

Printed at Gomer Press,
Llandysul, Ceredigion

Contents

FOREWORD

When I was asked to take an English-medium W.E.A. class on the history of Welsh literature, my first instinct was to refuse outright. There I was, with no academic qualifications, no prepared notes, certainly no love of holding forth before a group of strangers. What knowledge I did have was the result of voracious but quite undisciplined reading for my own pleasure. To accept seemed to me at the time to be the ultimate in effrontery and foolhardiness.

But accept I did, being persuaded that my very lack of academic background could make communication easier. Whether this was so or not I cannot tell, but those winter weeks, repeated the following year, came to be among the most rewarding of my life, for communication works both ways. Perhaps I was particularly fortunate in my classes, a varied cross-section of mainly English 'settlers', anxious to know as much as possible about the history and literature of their adopted country.

I was grateful for their enthusiasm and loyalty, and, together, we embarked on a voyage of discovery. When, eventually, it was suggested to me by the organizer, Cyril Jones, that others might enjoy a 'popular' introduction to Welsh literature based on my notes, I had no difficulty this time in agreeing, particularly when Emeritus Professor Geraint Gruffydd, the eminent Welsh scholar, promised to oversee the finished volume for any glaring errors or misapprehensions (though, in the event, he did far more than that). My gratitude for his interest is unbounded. My thanks also to the staff of the Dolgellau Centre of Gwynedd County Library for their patience and invaluable assistance.

Attempting to give readers a taste of Welsh literature from the sixth century to the present-day based on ten lectures meant an uncomfortable degree of selectivity. My choice of *llenorion* was entirely personal and uncomprehensive. I certainly don't expect to escape criticism for omissions.

7

It goes without saying that this book would have been impossible without the previous work of a host of scholars, and I have tried to acknowledge not only their books by name but also any quoted passages. If inadvertently I've failed, I hope they will realise that this was quite unintentional. I was particularly fortunate in being able to refer to the invaluable Writers of Wales series, published by the University of Wales Press.

Finally, the title. Not so long ago a prominent (ex) Minister of the Crown spoke somewhat dismissively of Welsh being 'a private language'. I hope this small volume will convince others, if not the gentleman himself, that it is considerably more than that.

THE BEGINNING

Welsh literature began in the sixth century. To state that baldly is, of course, a very dangerous thing to do. For centuries there has been a lot of disagreement about this, partly because the dividing line between what was called Brittonic speech and Welsh was difficult to assess. However, by now there is general agreement that the earliest reference to poetry composed in the Welsh language is found in the work of a cleric called Gildas— *De Excidio et Conquestu Britanniae* . . . written probably around the middle of the sixth century.

Gildas was not very complimentary. He referred to 'the voice of a rascally crew yelling forth, like Bachanalian revellers, full of lies and foaming phlegm, so as to besmear everyone near them.'

A.O.H. Jarman points out that these words refer to the bards of Maelgwn Gwynedd's court. (Maelgwn's great-grandfather, Cunedda Wledig, had come to Gwynedd with his eight sons from Manaw in the Firth of Forth, or so the Gwynedd historians thought.) The bards were only performing their duty of singing the praise of their ruler, which was their sole function. One could say that they were the P.R.s of their day. The language in which they composed was almost certainly an early form of Welsh, which was now taking shape after the break-up of Brittonic speech spoken by the Britons.

It may surprise you to know that most of the earliest Welsh poetry was written on the borders of Scotland and England, i.e. Strathclyde (Glasgow), Rheged (Carlisle), Gododdin (Edinburgh) and Elfed (Leeds), during the time of troubles following the withdrawal of the Roman legions from Britain. The Anglo-Saxons had already conquered large tracts of south-east Britain, and the decisive separation of the Britons of Wales from those of the north is dated from the middle of the seventh century. Gildas accused the Britons of quarrelling among themselves and listening to the vanities of their poets instead of keeping to the narrow path of Christian unity and obedience.

The poet had then a traditional status in society. It is hard for

9

us today to appreciate that all this praising of great lords could be anything other than downright flattery, but, according to Anthony Conran, translator of much of the early verse, this is a distortion of the truth. The *prifardd* (chief poet) retained his mystery. If his poetry was any good his own artistic individuality would emerge, not as a piece of special pleading in order to curry favour with a difficult patron. There were limits, of course, and a certain technical formalism was demanded, but the individual poet was given quite a lot of freedom.

A word here about translating poetry. We all realise that a great deal is inevitably lost in translation. As Professor Gwyn Thomas has pointed out, words meaning the same thing vary in length in different languages, for example *bara*—bread, *ystáfell*—room, *gogledd*—north. This can obviously affect the rhythm of a line of poetry. If you've ever had to translate the words of a song, you will know exactly what I mean.

Then there is the accent. In Welsh the accent is usually on the penultimate syllable. This is not so in English, for example *ohérwydd*—because, *ffurfáfen*—firmament. And again if you've ever tried rhyming using the exact translation you will soon have discovered this is well-nigh impossible.

What the translator aims to do is convey the essence of the poem as best he can. It is so easy to render a good line in the original language into something commonplace in another. Translating the strict metrical form of Welsh poetry, called *cynghanedd*, obviously has its own hazards.

The love of form is a predominant feature of early Welsh poetry. *Cynghanedd* might be described as a very sophisticated form of alliteration, sometimes combined with internal rhyme. In the earliest Welsh poetry it was used in a rudimentary form, and did not become fully developed until the Middle Ages.

The early poets are called the *Cynfeirdd*, and the name seems to have been first used by the Dolgellau antiquary, Robert Vaughan of Hengwrt (1592-1667), who gave the title *Y Cynfeirdd Cymreig* to a manuscript collection he had assembled of old or early Welsh poetry. Later on, in the twelfth and thirteenth centuries, these were succeeded by the *Gogynfeirdd*, which translates, rather piquantly I think, as Fairly Early Poets, apparently an eighteenth-century designation to suggest that the older verse still survived.

The two names known to us today as the most important of the *Cynfeirdd* are Taliesin and Aneirin. Their work (or perhaps I should say their presumed work) is found in two medieval manuscripts known as the Book of Taliesin, written in *c*. 1350 (MS. in the National Library, Aberystwyth), and the Book of

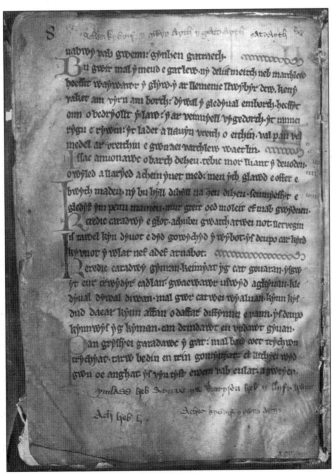

A page from the Book of Aneirin

11

Aneirin, written *c.* 1250 (MS. in the South Glamorgan County Library, Cardiff).

Taliesin's work is associated with the court of Urien, king of Rheged, which is thought to have been at Carlisle. Aneirin was court poet to a kingdom known as the Gododdin at Edinburgh (Din Eidyn).

The works of both are consistent with the general picture agreed by modern scholars of northern Britain in the Dark Ages. So this tends to confirm the view that poetry was composed in a form of Welsh as early as the second half of the sixth century. It is now generally agreed that the language had been in existence long enough for poets of the stature of Taliesin and Aneirin to regard it as a worthy medium for their own work.

Kennneth Jackson, a leading authority on the linguistic history of the period, says,

> One can say that the Welsh language, in the form of primitive Welsh, had come into existence not by the first, but certainly by the second half of the 6th century, and the poems of Taliesin and Aneirin, in Welsh, not British, could have been composed towards the end of that century.

But Dr Jackson still refers to the Gododdin as 'the oldest Scottish poem'!

What sort of poems were they? Christianity had already reached these parts, as we can see from references to God, heaven, communion, altars, churches and penance. But, of course, it was the earthly lord rather than the heavenly lord who got the praise in the poems of Aneirin and Taliesin. It was their lord's bravery and the virtue of loyalty that were emphasised. The lord gave the warrior food and drink, thus binding him to service unto death. This was called *talu medd*, that is, the payment of mead, or 'to be worth his mead'.

It must be admitted that we have no contemporary evidence for the existence of either Taliesin or Aneirin. All we have are the poems themselves, and scholars, in the main, don't dispute the authenticity of these (although there are exceptions!). If you would like to know more, then read Professor Jarman's book in the Writer of Wales series, in addition, of course, to the *Guide to Welsh Literature* which he edited with Gwilym Rees Hughes.

There are some 60 compositions in the Book of Taliesin, of which about 15 belong to *Hanes Taliesin* (The Tale of Taliesin). In this the poet is portrayed as a character in a saga. No one knows who exactly the historic poet was, but Sir Ifor Williams suggests that as a young man he lived in Powys, for his earliest known poem was addressed to Cynan Garwyn, king of Powys. So this, concludes Sir Ifor, is the earliest surviving poem in the Welsh language. In Taliesin's time Powys was much bigger than it is today, stretching right up through England towards the Old North.

Taliesin had heard of the exploits and bravery of Urien, king of Rheged in the Old North, and went to him to become his bard. The Anglo-Saxon enemy had settled in the north-east of England where their two kingdoms were called Deifr and Brynaich. Taliesin's poem tells of Urien and his son Owain fighting this enemy.

Scholarship is a funny business, theories among scholars differing so widely. Another scholar, David Kirby, does not agree with Sir Ifor Williams's interpretation, arguing that Taliesin must have moved from the Old North, i.e. Rheged, to Powys, rather than the other way round. A clue to this is in the many place-names in the poems. Apart from those in the poems to Cynan, they are nearly all in the Old North. As in the Book of Aneirin, the writing is very direct with sparing use of literary devices such as metaphors. Instead, they express as clearly as possible what exactly was meant, and once, having said it, leave it at that without embellishment. They painted pictures rather than described emotions.

In his poems to Urien of Rheged, the king is praised as protector of his people as well as for his qualities as a warrior. Taliesin's portrait of Urien has been described as the poet's greatest achievement. One poem tells of an encounter between Urien, his son Owain and their men, with a hostile army led by a leader named Fflamddwyn (the Flamebearer); see 'The Battle of Argoed Llwyfain', page 18-19.

Erechwydd, named in the poem, has been identified as Yorkshire, the Eastlands as Northumbria. One thing special about it is its dramatic quality. The actors' words are quoted directly—Fflamddwyn's demand for the surrender of hostages, Owain's defiant refusal, and Urien's call to his men to attack the enemy.

It appears that on one occasion Taliesin was *persona non grata* with Urien, perhaps because he had written poems in praise of a rival king. To make amends Taliesin wrote his poem 'Dadolwch' (Reconciliation).

It must be remembered that later on, between the ninth and thirteenth centuries, another writer made Taliesin himself the chief character of a legendary saga, depicting him as a seer surpassing all other men in wisdom and knowledge. As I've already mentioned, some of the poems which incorporate the saga are included in the Book of Taliesin.

A later story tells how the poet got his name:

A witch called Ceridwen lived on the shores of Bala lake. Her son Morfran was said to be the ugliest man in the world, and his mother, feeling sorry for him, decided to make him the cleverest man in the world. First she boiled a cauldron of herbs which could give him all knowledge. To help her she got a young boy called Gwion Bach from Llanfair Caereinion to keep stirring the pot while she looked for herbs. At the end of a year she was so weary she decided to take a rest, leaving Gwion and Morfran to tend the cauldron. Once on their own, Gwion pushed Morfran aside and took his place. The pot boiled over and some drops of the mixture fell on his finger. When he sucked it he immediately became the wisest person in the world, and ran away. Ceridwen woke up, saw what happened and gave chase. Gwion changed himself into a hare, and this started off a series of changes, Ceridwen becoming a greyhound, then an otter, then a hawk and eventually a black hen. By this time Gwion himself had had several changes ending up as a grain of wheat, which the black hen gobbled up, and Ceridwen once more became a woman. Nine months later Gwion was reborn as her son. She straight away put him in a bag and threw him into a river. A young prince found the bag in the Dyfi estuary. When he saw the beautiful child inside he exclaimed, '*Dyma dal iesin!*' (What a lovely forehead!) The child at once replied, '*Taliesin bid!*' (Let it be Taliesin.)

Let's now turn to Aneirin and his poem 'Y Gododdin'. The Gododdin lived in the country around Edinburgh (Din Eidyn) and their king was Mynyddawg. He and his people were constantly at war with the English in the south. At one time the English had taken possession of Catraeth (Catterick) which had been a Roman fort, and was therefore of strategic importance. (Another theory equates Catraeth with Richmond.) Mynyddawg decided to send his best army to regain it—three hundred young men of noble birth. This battle hasn't been recorded in any extant historical document, but it's reasonable to suppose that it was one of the many unrecorded battles fought *c*. 600 AD between the Britons of the north and the Angles of the east.

In the prologue, the work is described as 'a poem of the son of Dwywai'.

> Gododdin, I make my claim boldly on thy behalf
> In the presence of the throng in the court,
> With the lay of the son of Dwywai of high courage
> May it be manifest in the one place that it vanquishes
>   all others.
>
> Since the courteous one, the rampart of battle was slain
> Since the earth covered Aneirin,
> Poetry and the men of Gododdin are now parted.
> (Trans. K. Jackson)

Professor Jarman says that this Dwywai was also the mother of Deiniol, founder saint of Bangor. If Aneirin was the younger brother of Deiniol he would have been related to many of the leading figures of the Old North, including Urien Rheged himself.

According to the poem, the three hundred warriors spent a whole year at Mynyddawg's court preparing for battle, drinking their lord's mead and learning military discipline. They were mostly men of the Gododdin kingdom, but some had come from other Brythonic areas, including parts of north Wales.

The mead, as we have seen, had great symbolic significance, with *talu medd* being treated as a token of the bond between the chieftain and his warrior. But obviously going to war after drinking mead for a year has its own repercussions.

15

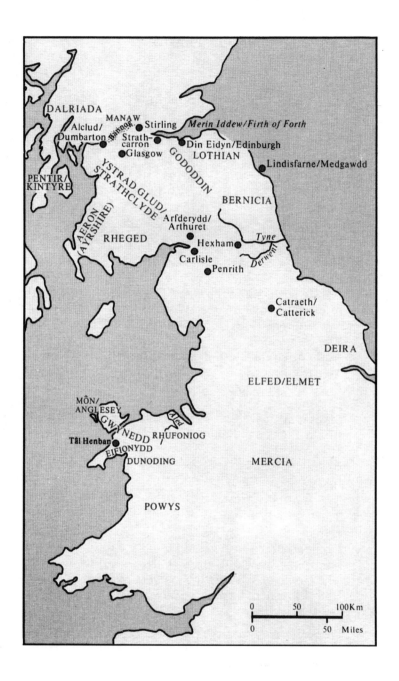

The poem described how the band set out for the dangerous place where they knew their enemies lay in wait for them. They were sorely outnumbered and, after a week's fighting, every member but one of Mynyddawg's army was slain, leaving Catraeth in English hands; see 'Y Gwŷr a aeth Gatraeth . . .', page 20.

The poem was careful not to stress the futility of it all or the waste. Instead it sang of heroic glory. True the mead Mynyddawg had given his men proved poison, but it was all in a good cause. The poet's song to valour and heroism was more valid than ever.

So the Gododdin is not an elegy. Professor Jarman calls it a poem of celebration, celebration not only of the martial qualities of the heroes, but also of their devotion to the concept of honour and renown in battle at whatever cost. It is the only complete exposition of the heroic ideal in Welsh literature. While Taliesin's poems are full of praise for martial qualities, they don't credit the warriors with the readiness found in the Gododdin to fight until death for their king. Taliesin's poems are more varied. They include dramatic monologue and dialogue. The Gododdin could perhaps seem repetitive and monotonous except for its great linguistic richness, remarkable in those early years of Welsh literature.

But for us, perhaps, the most interesting poem of all in the ancient period is one which, by a fortunate blunder, found its way into the Book of Aneirin in the middle of the Gododdin. It would seem to be a kind of nursery rhyme, written in the margin of some old copy of Aneirin's poems, which someone else, in copying, incorporated into the text without realising what it was; see 'Pais Dinogad', page 21.

TALIESIN

BRWYDR ARGOED LLWYFAIN

Ar fore Sadwrn cad fawr a fu
O pan gododd yr haul hyd dywyllu.
Ymosododd Fflamddwyn yn bedwar llu;
A Goddau a Rheged wrthi'n ymgasglu
I Ddyfwy, o Argoed hyd Arfynydd—
Ni chaent ymdroi hyd yn oed undydd.
Galwodd Fflamddwyn, y mawr ei drybestod,
'A roddir y gwystlon, a ydynt yn barod?'
Atebodd Owain, dwyrain drallod,
'Ni roddir. Nid oeddynt, nid ydynt barod.
A disgynnydd o Goel a fyddai'n flinderog
Iawn cyn y talai'n wystl yr un o'i gydnabod.'
Galwodd Urien, arglwydd Erechwydd,
'Am ein teulu, os bydd cad o'u herwydd,
Dyrchafwn darianau yn uchel ar fynydd
A chodwn wynebau uwchben yr ymyl
A dyrchafwn wayw uwchben gwŷr;
A chyrchwn ar Fflamddwyn yn ei luoedd
A thrawwn hwn a'i holl finteioedd.'

    Ac o flaen Argoed Llwyfain
    Bu llawer celain,
    Cochai brain ar ryfel wŷr.

    A'r gwŷr a gyrchodd gyda'u harglwydd—
    Bwriadaf roi blwyddyn gron i'w clodydd.

    A than y nychaf fi'n hen
    Yn nygn angen angau
    Ni byddaf fi'n llawen
    Oni folaf fi Urien.

(Diweddariad Gwyn Thomas)

THE BATTLE OF ARGOED LLWYFAIN

There was a great battle Saturday morning
From when the sun rose until it grew dark.
The fourfold hosts of Fflamddwyn invaded,
Goddau and Rheged gathered in arms,
Summoned from Argoed as far as Arfynydd—
They might not delay by as much as a day
With great swaggering din, Fflamddwyn shouted,
'Have these hostages come? Are they ready?'
To him then Owain, scourge of the eastlands,
'They've not come, no! They're not, nor shall they be ready!
And a whelp of Coel would indeed be afflicted
Did he have to give any man as a hostage!'
And Urien, lord of Erechwydd, shouted,
'If they would meet us now for a treaty
High on the hilltop let's raise our ramparts,
Carry our faces over the shield rims,
Raise up our spears, men, over our heads
And set upon Fflamddwyn in the midst of his hosts
And slaughter him, ay, and all that go with him!'

    There was many a corpse beside Argoed Llwyfain;
    From warriors ravens grew red,

    And with their leader a host attacked,
    For a whole year I shall sing to their triumph.

    And when I'm grown old, with death hard upon me,
    I'll not be happy unless I praise Urien.

                    (Trans. by Anthony Conran)

ANEIRIN

CATRAETH

Y gwŷr aeth i Gatraeth oedd ffraeth eu llu;
Ar lasfedd ymborthyn, a gwenwyn fu,
Trichannyn ar orchymyn yn ymgyrchu;
Ac wedi elwch, tawelwch fu.
Er myned i lannau ar benyd yn llu,
Angau yn ddiau oedd i'w trywanu

> Men went to Catraeth, keen was their company,
> They were fed on fresh mead, and it proved poison—
> Three hundred warriors ordered for warfare,
> And after the revelling, there was silence,
> Although they might go to the shrines to do penance,
> This much was certain, death would transfix them.

Y gwŷr aeth i Gatraeth gyda'r wawr
Byrhaodd eu natur eu bywyd yn fawr.
Medd yfent, melyn, melys, maglawr.
Am flwyddyn bu lawen lawer cerddor.
Coch eu clefyddau (nas purer!)
Gwyngalchog eu llafnau—pedeir hollt eu pennau
Ar faen gosgordd Mynyddog Mwynfawr.

> Men went to Catraeth with the dawn,
> Their fine spirit shortened their lives,
> Mead they drank, yellow, sweet and ensnaring:
> For that year many a minstrel was glad.
> Red their swords—may the blades not be cleaned!—
> White shields, and quadribarbed spearheads,
> In front of the host of Mynyddog Mwynfawr.

(Diweddariad Gwyn Thomas; trans. Anthony Conran)

PAIS DINOGAD

Pais Dinogad, un fraith fraith
O groen y bela y mae'r gwaith.

'Chwíd! Chwíd! Chwibanwaith.
Gwaeddwn ni, gwaeddant hwy—yr wyth gaeth.
Pan elai dy dad di i hela—
Gwayw ar ei ysgwydd, pastwn yn ei law—
Galwai ar gŵn tra bywiog,
'Giff! Gaff! Dal dal! Dwg dwg!'
Trywanai ef bysg o gorwg
Fel y trawa llew fân-filod!

Pan elai dy dad di i'r mynydd
Dygai ef un iwrch, un wyllt-hwch, un hydd,
Un rugiar fraith o fynydd,
Un pysgodyn o raeadr Derwennydd.
Beth bynnag a gyrhaeddai dy dad di â'i gigwain—
O wyllt-hwch, cadnoaid, creaduriaid—
Ni ddiangai'r un nad oedd rym i'w adain.

(Rhifau 79 ac 88 yn Canu Aneirin)
(Diweddariad Gwyn Thomas)

21

SONG TO A CHILD

Dinogad's smock is pied, pied—
Made it out of marten hide.
Whit, whit, whistle along,
Eight slaves with you sing the song.

When your dad went to hunt,
Spear on his shoulder, cudgel in hand,
He called his quick dogs, 'Giff, you wretch,
Gaff, catch her, catch her, fetch, fetch!'

From a coracle he'd spear
Fish as a lion strikes a deer.
When your dad went to the crag
He brought down roebuck, boar and stag,
Speckled grouse from the mountain tall
Fish from Derwent waterfall.

Whatever your dad found with his spear,
Boar or wild cat, fox or deer,
Unless it flew, would never get clear.

(Trans. Anthony Conran)

LLYWARCH HEN

Then followed what has been called the darkest age of Welsh poetry. Very little of it survived between the seventh and tenth centuries. But we do know quite a lot about the kings and princes during this period. For instance, there was Rhodri Mawr, king of Gwynedd from 844 to 878. Hywel Dda the law-maker was Rhodri's grandson, but, oddly enough, there is not one line of praise by a poet to either. This was a turbulent period, with continuous attacks on monasteries by the Danes who had settled in Ireland and elsewhere, so the manuscripts of many of these poems may have been lost in this way. Hywel Dda in his laws gave great prominence to poets, so it's fair to assume that their work from this time has nearly all been destroyed.

There are one or two poems which scholars say could have been composed about now, and there is reason to believe that the Song of Dinogad was one of them. There is also an elegy for Cynddylan ap Cyndrwyn. He was an historical king of Powys who was killed *c.* 655 and who was later to become a central figure in a series of saga poems. Cynddylan is a shadowy figure for the historian, but Melville Richards believed his court was on the Wrekin in Shropshire. It is this Elegy for Cynddylan that points the way to our next body of verse. This formed an important part of what is called Saga Literature.

I expect, when you read the words 'Saga Literature', you will immediately think of the Mabinogion and the tales of Arthur and his knights. One thing is rather strange. The title given to the most important tales in the Mabinogion is 'Pedair Cainc y Mabinogi', and they cover parts of Gwynedd, south-west (Dyfed) and south-east (Gwent) Wales. One may ask why Powys was omitted. Sir Ifor Williams suggested that a great body of prose saga literature here was lost. What we have got are poems about Powys composed in the ninth and tenth centuries describing events that took place in the sixth and early seventh century. Poems, but no prose.

By the ninth century, the Welsh had been pushed back and were now almost completely shut up behind Offa's Dyke, which, of course, had been built before King Offa of Mercia's death in 796. Quite naturally, in their deprivation, they turned to the stories of their old homes in Rheged, Elfed, Gododdin and the rich lands of eastern Powys. These are called the Songs of Llywarch Hen.

Llywarch Hen was an historical character from the sixth century and a contemporary of Taliesin. He is used in the poems as a fabled figure. Unfortunately, the prose and narrative parts of the saga are all lost. All we have are the sections in verse, when the story-teller used poetry and song to stress the dramatic and emotional nature of the speech of his characters. Sir Ifor Williams suggests that this is because, in the early oral stages of tradition, the minstrel knew the story by heart. There was no need for him to be able to repeat it word for word, provided he could bring in the *englynion* at the right moment. These, however, had to be carefully memorised. If he lacked confidence in his memory, all he had to do was to write the verses down on vellum, and in this way they were preserved intact for centuries. It should be added, however, that other scholars believe that these poems were independent works with little or no prose attached to them.

Although the poems are told in the first person, Llywarch Hen himself was not the author. He is a character in a drama. According to Sir Ifor Williams the poems are the finest example of the work of the early Welsh *cyfarwydd* (story-teller) and are in their way a masterpiece of dramatic art. It's tragic that only fragments have survived.

But who was the real Llywarch Hen? In early genealogies he is shown to have been a cousin of Urien Rheged, and he probably was a genuine sixth-century princeling. His father was Elidyr Lydanwyn, brother of Cynfarch, who was the father of Urien Rheged. Their mothers were also sisters, so his family connections were obviously impeccable.

There are three sections to the poems. First Llywarch's story, which in its present form is difficult to interpret, about the death of Urien Rheged. This is interspersed with nature poetry.

24

Then poems about Llywarch Hen himself and his relationsh. with his sons. And finally, the poems of Heledd, sister o Cynddylan lord of Powys.

Let's start with the one that tells of the fate of Llywarch's cousin, Urien Rheged, who had been killed in battle due to the treachery of another king, Morgan (see page 32). Llywarch had severed Urien's head from his body, apparently in order to prevent its desecration by the enemy. This was considered to be the last service one could render one's lord. Though it must be added that a recent critic has it that Llywarch was actually Urien's murderer, that he had killed him as a result of a feud and was now gripped by terrible remorse. The poem's latest editor, on the other hand, thinks that it stands outside the Llywarch Hen cycle altogether.

Be all that as it may, this is a good example of the kind of poem which makes you feel it's all about real people who knew genuine suffering. In fact, the greatest difference between the poems of Aneirin and Taliesin in the sixth century and these from the ninth is that the older poets ignored grief and calamity, and emphasised wholly their lords' valour. After all, that was what they were there for. The bond of *talu medd* had been made, ensuring them food and drink and other protection. Any act of shame following such generosity would be inconceivable.

There is a decided change when it comes to the poetry of Llywarch and Heledd. A doubt has seemingly crept in about old standards, and there is a subtle rejection of the whole heroic idea. Llywarch's twenty-four sons are killed in battle and Heledd's land and family are destroyed. While they are proud of all the heroism there is a hint of wondering about whether it has been worth all the killing and destruction. There is also in Llywarch's songs a certain idea of fate. One man is born happy and everything goes well for him throughout his life. Another, called a *diriaid* is born wretched, and he must accept that fate. 'He is a *diriaid* from birth,' says the poet. He is born with defects of character, whereas the other, the *dedwydd* is blessed, wise and his fate is good. As Professor Jarman has pointed out, this is rather like Blake's couplet:

25

Some are born to sweet delight
Some are born to endless night.

Although much more painful to read, there's no doubt that the Llywarch poems are more about what happens to real people with human failings than are those of his predecessors.

Llywarch has come from northern Britain to defend Powys, aided by his twenty-four sons. One by one all these sons are killed and Llywarch is left to become a homeless wanderer.

Perhaps the most interesting sequence in the series is a dramatic dialogue between Llywarch and one of his sons, Gwên. It is probably the earliest dialogue to have survived in Welsh literature. This is how Professor Jarman has analysed it.

All the sons have fallen except Gwên who has been at Urien's court in the north. Gwên has heard of his old father's plight and has come to Powys to help him. He announces his arrival with the strange words: 'My mother declares that I am thy son.' The implication being that the two have not met for a very long time. In his reply Llywarch both greets and reproaches him:

> I know from the elation in my heart
> That we are sprung from the same stock;
> Thou hast stayed away long, Oh, Gwên!

Gwên responds:

> My spear is sharp, flashing in the fight,
> I intend to guard the ford
> If I escape not, God be with thee.

A suggestion here that Gwên resents the reproach and is on the defensive.

Llywarch:
> If thou escapest, I shall see thee,
> If thou art slain, I shall weep for thee
> Lose not the honour of a man in the stress of battle.

Gwên:
> I shall not lose the honour of a warrior
> When brave men arm for the fray
> I shall endure hardship before I move from my post.

But the very idea of 'moving from one's post' would have been inconceivable to the Gododdin poet. For Llywarch it is equally unacceptable:

26

Llywarch: The wave runs along the shore
             Out of hand man's purpose fails
             In battle the ready of speech seek safety in flight.

Gwên replies truthfully:
             This I can say
             Spears will be shattered where I shall be
             I do not say that I shall not flee.

Llywarch continues to taunt his son:
             The horn that Urien gave thee
             With its golden baldric around its mouth
             Sound it if thou art hard pressed.

But Gwên ignores the taunt:
             In spite of fear before the warriors of England
             I shall not degrade myself
             I shall not awake the maidens.

Says Llywarch:
             When I was of the age of yonder youth
             Who wears spurs of gold
             Swiftly would I rush against the spear.

The exasperated Gwên replies:
             Thou livest, thy witness is dead
             No old man was ever a weakling in his youth.

Dr Jenny Rowland, in the most recent book on the Saga poetry, makes this interesting point:

This self-deception about his heroic past is the direct cause of Llywarch's tragedy in the Saga. His reputation as an undaunted champion, it must be remembered, depends solely on his own testimony; throughout he is shown as long past his prime. Although undoubtedly he was at one time a warrior, it appears that in looking back he vastly inflates his past deeds, inflating in turn present expectations for his sons. He urges them to do no less than what he claims to have done himself. But the odds are against Llywarch having performed what he claims to have done since he has survived to old age while all 24 of his sons are killed in youth. 'Marwnad Gwên' (his elegy on the death of Gwên) shows that the death of his last surviving son awakened him to the reality of his exaggerated expectation.

27

To continue Professor Jarman's translation and analysis:

> Four and twenty sons had I,
> Golden-torqued leading a host
> Gwên was the best of them

> Four and twenty sons in Llywarch's household
> Of brave fierce warriors;
> Too much renown is evil.

> Four and twenty sons bred of my body,
> Because of my tongue they have been slain.
> A little renown is good; they have been lost.

His mood is now one of disillusionment. Nothing remains and he is now an old man. The concluding scene of the Llywarch Hen Saga is a poem of twenty-one stanzas called 'Lament in Old Age'. It shows Llywarch living as a cowherd, subsisting on acorns. He is a wanderer rejected by all, deprived of his possessions, old, enfeebled, incapable. He remembers the splendid days of his youth, only to find that the pursuit of honour and renown is an insubstantial thing:

> Cyn crymu'n gefn-faglog bûm hy:
> Cawn groeso ymhob plasty
> Ym Mhowys, paradwys Cymru.

> Cyn crymu'n gefn-faglog bûm (ŵr) glân;
> Fy ngwayw ar flaengyrch oedd gyntaf ei gwân;
> Rwy'n gefngrwm, rwy'n drwm, rwy'n druan.

> Before my back was bent I was bold
> I was welcomed in the royal hall
> Of Powys, paradise of Wales.

> Before my back was bent I was handsome,
> My spear was first in battle, it led the attack,
> Now I am bowed, I am heavy, I am sad.

The lament, despite showing him as being self-centred and querulous, reveals him also as being mercilessly honest about himself. Moreover, throughout the series of *englynion*, it is, as Professor Jarman says, the work of a poet, one concerned with

28

questions and doubts about the nature of war, heroism and cowardice. He says that for the poets of the Gododdin such problems did not exist; but in effect the portrait drawn by the author of the Llywarch Hen poems is a rejection of the whole heroic ethos. Professor Jarman refers to the medieval Chanson de Roland where the hero is bitterly criticized by Ganelon for the selfishness which for years led him to sacrifice the flower of the manhood of France in order to meet the insatiable demands of his own pride. This was also a hero who refused to sound his horn to summon aid.

(It is fair to point out that the poems' latest editor, Jenny Rowland, would tend to disagree with this point of view. She, for instance, stresses the role of fate in the Llywarch saga.)

But now we come to the Heledd poems, another series of 113 *englynion* (in which Llywarch Hen does not appear). These deal with the fate of Cynddylan of Powys and his family, and the destruction of his court at Pengwern in the seventh century. Pengwern has been traditionally associated with Shrewsbury, but as we have seen, the Wrekin is favoured by a recent authority. But Ifor Williams thinks it might even be Trewern, near Welshpool, and, as he said, the Long Mynd Mountain would have made a fine platform for Heledd's lament.

Heledd, like Llywarch Hen, speaks in the first person. She was not the author, but a quasi-historical person, sister of Cynddylan, who was killed in battle with the men of Mercia, defending Trenn. This today is the name given to the river Tern in Shropshire. Cynddylan was buried in Baschurch (Eglwysau Basa). Heledd calls on women to come and gaze upon the desolate land as she mourns her brother in some of the most famous lines in Welsh literature. She stands on one of the neighbouring heights looking down on the blazing ruins of her home. In a long series of *englynion* she laments the destruction of Pengwern and the white homestead in the valley. She mourns the death of her eight sisters and seven brothers, and her own wretched fate, comparing it with the luxury of the old days. Where once she rode noble steeds and wore garments of scarlet bedecked with yellow plumes, she now had to sleep on rough goatskin.

Here is the rest of Anthony Conran's vivid description:

She watches in terror as an eagle feasts upon Cynddylan's dead body in the woods. She does not dare to go near, in case the birds turn on her. She has seen them before, these eagles fishing in the estuaries; now they swim in blood. She thinks of her victorious enemy, the one that slew Cynddylan; the eagles are pampered by him, and he prospers.

Then she looks up, hears another eagle scream and hover in the sky, talons down for the swoop. It is jealous of the flesh that she loves and would like to save, and jealous of its rival's feast. Her splintered mind remembers Trenn, the luckless, glittering town, that Cynddylan died defending, and the eyes of the eagles watch on the blood.

Heledd then sings an elegy to her sister, Ffreuer, who presumably died during the burning of Pengwern, in which she says that Ffreuer is lucky not to have lived to see the ruin of her land and family.

Then she cries out in agony that she herself is responsible for these disasters, for the burning of Eglwysau Basa, for the death of her brothers. Everything is due to the misfortunes of her own tongue.

The subject of moral guilt is introduced in a few stanzas:

Through the mischarge of my tongue have they been slain

Some specific act of selfishness on the part of Heledd and her sisters is suggested in the last *englyn* of the series:

I and Ffreuer and Medlan
Though there be war on every hand
We are not concerned; our people will not be killed.

The destruction of Pengwern is seen here as a punishment:

At the time when I lived sumptuously
I would not rise to give help
To a man sick of the pestilence.

Ultimately, like Llywarch, Heledd becomes a homeless wanderer, half demented, brooding over a vanished past:

30

I am called wild Heledd
Oh God! To whom will be given
My brothers' horses and their lands?

Jenny Rowland says that the disaster Heledd holds herself responsible for is on a far greater scale than Llywarch's loss of family: the greatest evidence for her overwhelming pride would be attributing such importance to herself, blaming herself for the destruction of Powys because of lapses in perfect Christian behaviour. Another interesting point Dr Rowland makes is that while Heledd's personal grief and love for her brother are evident, it is grief for the ruler which is stressed. Sorrow for her destroyed homeland is connected with a land lamenting its lost sovereignty. There is a great emphasis on the loss of the rightful ownership of the land. There is much interest today, she says, in *Canu Heledd*, and the link between the loss of Welsh sovereignty in the border region and the steady erosion of Welsh culture and language has contemporary parallels.

We are left wishing to know more, much more about these people in the Llywarch Saga. Sir Ifor Williams, I think, rightly claims for Heledd a place side by side with the Irish Deirdre of the Sorrows.

URIEN'S HEAD

I bear a head against my side,
He was an attacker between two hosts;
The proud son of Cynfarch owned it.

I bear a head against my side,
The head of generous Urien, he ruled a host,
And upon his white breast a black raven.

I bear a head against my left side,
Better would he be living than in the grave.
He was a refuge for the aged.

My arm is out of joint, my bosom is agitated,
My heart is broken.
I bear a head which sustained me.

*   *   *

The slender comely body is buried today
Beneath earth and a monument.
Alas my hand that my lord has been struck.

The slender comely body is buried today
Beneath earth and sand.
Alas my hand the fate that has befallen me.

(Trans. A. O. H. Jarman)

STAFELL GYNDDYLAN

Stafell Gynddylan, ys tywyll heno,
Heb dân, heb wely,
Wylaf dro, tawaf wedyn.

The hall of Cynddylan is dark tonight,
No fire, no bed,
I sometimes weep, then am silent.

Stafell Gynddylan, ys tywyll heno
Heb dân, heb gannwyll.
Ond am Dduw, pwy rydd im bwyll?

The hall of Cynddylan is dark tonight,
No fire, no candle
Who but God will give me peace?

Stafell Gynddylan, aethost wan dy wedd
Mae mewn bedd dy darian
Tra fu, nid briw'r glwyd yn unman.

The hall of Cynddylan, you are become wan,
Your shield is in the grave,
While he lived, no door needed bar.

Stafell Gynddylan, ys tywyll heno,
Heb dân, heb gerddau,
Cystudd ar ddeurudd yw'r dagrau.

The hall of Cynddylan is dark tonight,
No fire, no song.
Tears have withered my cheeks.

(Diweddariad Gwyn Thomas;
trans. Joseph P. Clancy)

Y DREF WEN

Y dref wen ym mron y coed,
  Sef yw ei harfer erioed
Ar wyneb ei gwellt y gwaed.

Y dref wen yn ei goror—
  Llwyd feddau yw ei harfer,
Gwaed o dan draed y gwŷr.

Y dref wen yn y dyffryn,
(Llawen y dideimlad ar gythrwfwl cad)
  Ei phobl a ddarfuan'.

Y dref wen rhwng Trenn a Throdwydd,
Mwy arferol tarian dwll yn dod o gad
  Nag ych ar nawn yn llonydd.

Y dref wen rhwng Trenn a Thrafal,
Mwy arferol y gwaed ar wyneb ei gwellt
  Nag aredig braenar.

(Diweddariad Gwyn Thomas)

THE WHITE TOWN

White town in the woodland's breast
Your bounty forever is this,
Blood on the face of the grass.

White town within this province,
Your bounty, green mementoes,
The blood that's beneath men's feet.

White town within the valley,
Festive the kites in battle's butchery,
The people have perished.

White town between Trenn and Trodwydd,
More common were torn shields from combat
Than oxen at mid-day.

White town between Trenn and Trafal,
More common was blood on the field's face
Than ploughing of fallow.

(Trans. Joseph P. Clancy)

ERYR ELI

Eryr Eli cryf ei lef heno,
Llyncodd ef ddiod waedlin,
Gwaed calon Cynddylan Wyn.

Eryr Eli, cryf-elwi heno,
Yng ngwaed gwŷr ymdreigli,
'Fe yng nghoed: loes oeda imi.

Eryr Eli a glywaf heno,
Gwaedlyd yw; nis heriaf.
'Fe yng nghoed: loes oeda arnaf.

Eryr Eli, dristed yw heno
Ddyffryn Meisir edmygwyd,
Tir Brochfael—hir y'i poenwyd.

Eryr Eli, gwylia'r moroedd—
Ni threiddia pysgod i'r aberoedd,
Geilw am waed gwŷr yn wleddoedd.

Eryr Eli, teithia'r coed heno,
Rhy fore ciniawa.
Llwydda traha'r sawl a'i bwyda.

(Diweddariad Gwyn Thomas)

EAGLE OF ELI

Eagle of Eli, loud its cry tonight—
Had drunk of a pool of blood,
The heart's blood of Cynddylan Wyn.

Eagle of Eli, it cried out tonight,
It swam in men's blood,
There in the trees! And I've misery on me.

Eagle of Eli, I hear it tonight,
Bloodstained it is, I dare not go near it—
There in the trees! I've misery on me.

Eagle of Eli that watches the seas,
In the estuaries fishes no longer.
It feasts on the blood of men.

Eagle of Eli walks in the wood tonight;
Too soon it has supped.
Who feeds it, his arrogance prospers.

(Trans. Anthony Conran)

SOME OTHER EARLY POETRY

Gnomic Poems

Before turning to prose works, let's look briefly at three more branches of poetry practised by the bards. First, something called Gnomic Poetry. This is how the Oxford English Dictionary defines the word gnomic: poetry used without past sense to express a general truth. Not very easy to understand, perhaps? Let's try again. A gnomic statement is something that is always true, not just true on one particular occasion. For instance, to say 'water is wet' is obviously true, but 'the fields are wet with dew' only happens at certain times. A truism notices things and draws conclusions that create some order in life.

It was the custom of early poets to string together gnomic sayings in *englynion*, each *englyn* beginning with the same word or expression. The pattern was usually, though not always, two lines about nature followed by one about man:

> Mountain snow, each region white — (a description)
> Common the raven calling — -do-
> No good comes of too much slumber — (a gnome)

As you can see, gnomes may also apply to behaviour, though Thomas Parry says that a gnome is not the same as a proverb, however much the two may resemble each other, even though it's true that the distinction is slight at times.

> Lovely the tips of the oaks, bitter the ash top
> Sweet the cow-parsnip, there's laughter in the wave,
> The cheek conceals not the grief of the heart.

Kenneth Jackson says that this kind of poetry can be explained by man's simple interest in his environment, in the living and inanimate objects of nature, and in the behaviour of his fellow-men—the sum of the experience that comes from observation, an expression of rustic wisdom. Not that the

38

product is folk poetry. These poems, he says, were sung by poets of lesser importance, perhaps by apprentices in the bardic schools (though this view is now disputed). What is particularly interesting to us today is Professor Jackson's suggestion that these truisms about nature form the early basis of the study of physics, botany and zoology.

Nature Poems

The poet's interest in nature was simple and straightforward. One of the most primitive methods of using nature in poetry was in riddling verse (*cerdd ddyfalu*), that is, a description of an object, giving all its particular characteristics, without actually naming it. For instance:

> Guess who it is: created before the Flood,
> A creature strong, without flesh, without bone,
> Without veins, without blood, without head, without feet,
> It grows no older, it grows no younger than it began . . .
> Tis on sea, tis on land, it sees not, is not seen;
> It is evil, it is good, it is yonder, it is here.

Did you guess? The answer, of course, is the wind. Here is another nature poem:

> Lovely are fruits in time of harvest,
> And lovely also is wheat on the haulm,
> Lovely is an eagle on the seashore when the tide's at the full,
> And lovely also are seagulls at play . . .
>
> Lovely is May to cuckoos and nightingale,
> Lovely also it is when the weather is fair,
> Lovely is a garden of herbs when its leeks thrive,
> Lovely also is charlock in the sprouting,
> Lovely is heather when it grows ruddy,
> Lovely also the sea-marsh for the cattle.

It ends with a religious couplet:

> Loveliest it is of all loveliness
> To be at one with God on Judgement Day.
>
> (Trans. H. Idris Bell)

39

When things looked black for the Welsh nation, poets would try to raise the spirits of their fellow countrymen by singing about its revival. This revival would be associated with the name of some hero or other, who would return to make the country invincible.

This hero would be one of the great names of the past—Arthur, Cynan, Cadwaladr, Owain. The people were persuaded that their hero was not dead but in hiding somewhere, and that, one day, he would come to deliver them. This kind of poetry was practised in Wales between the ninth and the fifteenth centuries. Two names in particular were invoked, that of Taliesin and that of Myrddin (Merlin).

I've already recounted one of the legends of Taliesin. This is the legend of Myrddin:

About the year 575 the chieftain Rhydderch Hen had gained a victory over another Brittonic king, Gwenddolau, in a battle near Carlisle. According to this legend, Myrddin had fought on the side of Gwenddolau, and, in the course of the battle, had lost his reason. He had fled to the wood of Celyddon (Caledonia), and there he lived for fifty years with no company save for the trees and wild beasts, mourning the slaying of Gwenddolau. But along the years, his madness had helped him acquire the gift of prophecy. Some modern psychologists like R. D. Laing would no doubt recognise this phenomenon. There are similar tales in Ireland and Scotland.

The oldest prophecy now in existence is called *Armes Prydain* (The Presage of Britain). It is thought to belong to the year 930. In it there are complaints about the stewards of Cirencester and their unreasonable taxes. It calls for a confederation against the English and has a vision of their headlong expulsion through Sandwich into the sea. The leaders of this battle will be two heroes called Cynan and Cadwaladr, and in the end they will rule the whole of England and Wales. No one knows who this Cynan was, but Cadwaladr was the son of Cadwallon, the Welsh king, who conquered Northumbria in the seventh century.

Examples of Gnomic Poetry

Llym awel, llwm bryn, anodd caffael clyd;
Llifa'r rhyd, rhewa'r llyn;
Fe saif gŵr ar un gwelltyn.

> Wind piercing, hill bare, hard to find shelter;
> Ford turns foul, lake freezes,
> A man could stand on a stalk.

Ton ar don yn toi y tir;
Uchel y gwaeddau ger uchel fannau'r bryn;
Prin, allan, y sefir.

> Wave on wave cloaks countryside;
> Shrill the shrieks from the peaks of the mountain;
> One can scarce stand outside.

Trist oer (y) llyn rhag twrw'r gaea',
Crin (y) cawn, gwellt druana,
Llidiog awel, coed yn dena.

> Cold the lake-bed from winter's blast;
> Dried reeds, stalks broken;
> Angry wind, woods stripped naked

Eira mynydd, gwyn pob tu,
Cynefin brân a chanu.
Ni ddaw da o dra-chysgu.

> Mountain snow, each region white;
> Common the raven calling
> No good comes of too much slumber.

Eira mynydd, gwyn ceunant,
Rhag rhuthr gwynt y gwydd a wyrant;
Llawer dau a ymgarant
A byth ni chyfarfyddant.

> Mountain snow, deep dingle white;
> Woods bend before wind's onslaught;
> Many couples are in love
> And never come together.

(Trans. Joseph P. Clancy)

41

SOURCES AND FURTHER READING

A.O.H. Jarman. *The Cynfeirdd*. University of Wales Press (Writers of Wales series).

A.O.H. Jarman and Gwilym Rees Hughes, editors. *A Guide to Welsh Literature*. Vol. I, Christopher Davies.

Thomas Parry. *A History of Welsh Literature*. Trans. H. Idris Bell. Oxford University Press.

—*The Introduction to the Oxford Book of Welsh Verse*.

Gwyn Jones. *The Oxford Book of Welsh Verse in English*.

Anthony Conran. *The Penguin Book of Welsh Verse*.

Joseph P. Clancy. *The Earliest Welsh Poetry*. Macmillan.

Ifor Williams. (ed. Rachel Bromwich) *The Beginning of Welsh Poetry*. Cardiff.

— (trans. J.E. Caerwyn Williams). *The Poems of Taliesin*. Dublin.

Kenneth Jackson. *The Gododdin*. Edinburgh University Press.

Jenny Rowland. *Early Welsh Saga Poetry*. D.S. Brewer.

THE MABINOGION

Time now for us to come to what is generally regarded as the greatest treasure of our literature, this collection of tales told by story-tellers over the centuries, found in two ancient manuscripts. There are eleven tales in all, preserved in the two books, The White Book of Rhydderch (c. 1350) and The Red Book of Hergest (c. 1400). In addition, there is the Peniarth manuscript which contains portions of different stories, some of them written down a hundred years before The White Book of Rhydderch.

As often happens, scholars disagree on dates of the original stories, Sir Ifor Williams placing them between 1055 and 1062; Saunders Lewis, between 1170 and 1190; and Thomas Charles Edwards between 1050 and 1120. Brynley Roberts says there could have been as long a period as two centuries between the earliest and the latest. He points out that, altogether, they represent some of the chief themes of the story-world of the Middle Ages—religious myths in *Pedair Cainc y Mabinogi* (The Four Branches of the Mabinogi); historical myths in 'Lludd a Llefelys' and 'Breuddwyd Macsen'; a folk tale in 'Culhwch ac Olwen'; Arthurian chivalry in Peredur, Owein, and Gereint ac Enid; and, the most original of all, 'Breuddwyd Rhonabwy' (The Dream of Rhonabwy).

You may know that the Mabinogion were translated into English for the first time by Lady Charlotte Guest. The term 'Mabinogion' is, in fact, a misnomer based on an error, but it is convenient to use it to designate the collection of eleven tales together, the term 'Mabinogi' being correctly reserved for the group of four tales as *Pedair Cainc y Mabinogi*.

Lady Charlotte was an Englishwoman from Lincolnshire married to Sir Josiah Guest, master of the Dowlais ironworks. This remarkable woman had been given a copy of part of The Red Book of Hergest by a man called John Jones (bardic name, Tegid). He had copied it in the library of Jesus College, Oxford. She immediately set about translating it, and it was published

43

The First Branch of the Mabinogi—Pwyll prince of Dyfed—in The White Book of Rhydderch

44

in three volumes in 1846. Although she herself had certainly learnt Welsh very well, and had taught it to her children, she had to depend on the help of more proficient translators when tackling this task. Her undoubted achievement was to have polished the translations into elegant English.

The title may be derived from the word *mab* meaning youth or son. Another theory says it is derived from the name of the Celtic god Mabon. It was first used to describe stories of boyhood, similar to the French word *enfance*. It told of the boyhood of Pryderi, but gradually this grew to encompass stories about all sorts of other people.

Of the eleven stories, undoubtedly the best known are *Pedair Cainc y Mabinogi*. The other seven, probably composed by a number of different authors, are called The Dream of Macsen Wledig; Lludd and Llefelys; Culhwch and Olwen (which is the earliest Arthurian tale in Welsh); The Dream of Rhonabwy; and three later Arthurian romances—The Lady of the Fountain, Peredur Son of Efrawg, and Geraint, Son of Erbin.

All the stories are court tales about people of the highest rank. Their pastimes are hunting, feasting, drinking and listening to the *cyfarwydd* (the traditional story-teller); all pastimes not too different from our own today, except that instead of a *cyfarwydd* we have television.

The *cyfarwydd* was a very important man. We have already seen how, at the courts of the princes, the poet was accorded a place of honour. Story-telling may have been one of his functions. In Ireland it was an even more honourable occupation with the story-teller having to learn 350 stories before he could be considered qualified. There's nothing to tell us how the Welsh story-teller learnt his art, but he would probably have been apprenticed to experienced masters.

There have, of course, been other translations apart from that of Lady Charlotte Guest, notably a very fine one made some years ago by Professors Gwyn Jones and Thomas Jones for Everyman's Library, and the examples I now quote are taken largely from this important work.

In one of the tales from the Four Branches Gwydion the magician says to Pryderi:

'Lord, it is a custom with us that the first night after one comes to a great man, the chief bard shall have the say. I will tell a tale gladly.'

Gwydion was the best teller of tales in the world. And that night he entertained the court with pleasant tales and story-telling till he was praised by everyone in the court, and it was a pleasure for Pryderi to converse with him.

Where did the old story-tellers get their material? Certainly not out of their own imagination. They didn't invent their characters or events, but drew on a wealth of stories inherited from a remote past of whose beginning they had no knowledge. Many of the characters are in origin old gods and godesses of Celtic mythology, with counterparts in early Irish saga. The story-tellers used the tales to show off their own art, no doubt embellishing them till at last there came some writer who gave them a final form on his parchment.

At least most scholars agree that the Four Branches is the work of a single man, a writer of the most brilliant kind. We don't know who he was. Some have said he must have been a monk, others a lawyer, some suggest an eleventh-century bishop of St. David's. He was, in any case, probably a native of sout-west Wales. Whoever he was, he was, above all, an artist of great skill and is even today an inspiration to many modern Welsh writers.

Although there are inconsistencies in the stories which may have occurred for all sorts of reasons, it is the author's style which is so superb. His prose flows smoothly and economically without a proliferation of alliteration. There are adjectives, of course, but these are restrained and there are no lengthy descriptive passages, no rhetorical language of the sort you find in other tales of the Mabinogion.

This is how the First Branch opens in the Everyman translation:

Pwyll prince of Dyfed was lord over the seven cantrefs of Dyfed: and once upon a time he was at Arberth, a chief court of his, and it came into his head and heart to go a-hunting. The part of his domain which it pleased him to hunt was Glyn Cuch. And he set out that night from Arberth, and came as far as Pen Llwyn

Diarwya, and there he was that night. And on the morrow in the young of the day he arose and came to Glyn Cuch to loose his dogs in the wood. And he sounded his horn and began to muster the hunt, and followed after the dogs and lost his companions; and whilst he was listening to the cry of the pack, he could hear the cry of another pack, but they had not the same cry, and were coming to meet his own pack.

And he could see a clearing in the wood as of a level field, and, as his pack reached the edge of the clearing, he could see a stag in front of the other pack. And, towards the middle of the pack, lo, the pack that was pursuing it, overtaking it and bringing it to the ground. And then he looked at the colour of the pack, without troubling to look at the stag; and of all the hounds he had seen in the world, he had seen no dogs the same colour as these. The colour that was on them was a brilliant, shining white, and their ears were red; and as the exceeding whiteness of the dogs glittered, so glittered the exceeding redness of their ears. And with that he came to the dogs, and drove away the pack that killed the stag, and baited his own pack upon the stag.

The story goes on. Just then he sees a horseman coming towards him, who challenges him for having baited his pack on the dead stag, and driven away the stranger's pack. Pwyll apologises profusely and offers to redeem his fault. The horseman then tells him he is Arawn, king of Annwn (the Otherworld). He says he wishes to rid himself of the oppression of a neighbour, King Hafgan, and Pwyll could win his friendship by agreeing to go to Annwn in his stead for a year, where 'the fairest lady thou didst ever see I will set to sleep with thee each night, and my form and semblance upon thee'.

He then explains that he has an appointment with Hafgan at the end of the year. Pwyll is to give him one blow, one only, but a blow which he will not survive. In the meantime Arawn will take Pwyll's place in his kingdom, saying that 'neither man nor woman in thy kingdom shall know I am not thou'.

So Pwyll spends a year in the Otherworld, ruling wisely and living chastely with Arawn's wife, who has no idea of the swap that has taken place. True she later confesses she had found her husband's behaviour in turning his back on her in bed somewhat bizarre. But all is explained at the end of the year when Pwyll defeats Hafgan and restores the Otherworld kingdom to Arawn.

The next scene in the story shows Pwyll sitting on a mound near Arberth in Dyfed when he sees a beautiful maiden ride by on a white horse. He sends his men to overtake her but, however hard they ride, they cannot catch up with her. Then Pwyll himself tries, but the same thing happens. She is always ahead of him although her pace is quite unhurried. At last, after several days of this, he calls out to her:

'Lady, for his sake whom thou lovest best, stay for me.'

Then stay she does, saying: 'I will, gladly, and it had been better for the horse hadst thou asked this long since.'

She then tells him she is the daughter of Hefeydd the Old, that she loves him, Pwyll, but has been promised in marriage to Gwawl. She suggests a plan whereby Gwawl is to be humiliated at their impending betrothal feast, and so forced to abandon his claim on her.

The plan succeeds. Rhiannon and Pwyll are married, and they have a son, Pryderi. But the child is stolen away by enchantment on the night of his birth. Rhiannon is accused of murdering the child, and for punishment she is made to sit every day near a horse-block outside the gate to tell her story to everyone who comes by, and offer any guest or stranger to carry him or her on her back into the court.

In his book on the Mabinogion in the Writers of Wales series, Professor Proinsias Mac Cana suggested that this is hardly the kind of story the author would have intended for himself had he had the choice, and that he betrays his slight discomfort by applying a touch of deodorant before and after. The passage opens with the statement that Rhiannon 'summoned to her teachers and wise men. And she preferred doing penance to wrangling with the women she took on her penance', the implication being that her penance was, in a sense, self-imposed; and the author closes by pointing out that, even though Rhiannon offered to carry visitors on her back, 'it was chance (*damwein*) that any one would permit himself to be carried'. A nice ambiguous phrase, says Mac Cana, that salves the conscience without ruining the point of the story.

All this goes on for some years, but the boy is eventually found and Rhiannon is reinstated. Pryderi grows to manhood and, on Pwyll's death, becomes Lord of Dyfed.

The Second Branch is Mabinogi Branwen. Matholwch, King of Ireland, comes to ask the hand in marriage of Branwen, sister of the great chieftain, Bendigeidfran. Bendigeidfran, a giant, who cannot be contained within a house, agrees and the marriage is consummated in Aberffraw in Anglesey. However, at the wedding there is a fly in the ointment in the shape of Efnisien, half-brother to Branwen, who is angry at not having been consulted about the wedding. In revenge he mutilates the Irish king's horses. Matholwch is only prevented from leaving immediately by Bendigeidfran's promise of abundant reparation and the gift of a magic cauldron.

Back in Ireland, Branwen eventually gives birth to a son, Gwern, and everything seems very happy. But after a year there's a kind of delayed reaction to the insult offered to Matholwch, and Branwen is imprisoned and cruelly treated. (The similarity to Rhiannon's story must interest feminists.)

Branwen's only companion is a starling which she trains and sends to Wales to tell her brother of her plight. He invades Ireland and there is a terrible war, with the Irish soon forced to retreat over the Shannon. Because of treachery following the treaty, the men of the 'Island of the Mighty' (Britain) are all killed, apart from seven who include Pryderi and Manawydan, Branwen's other brother. Bendigeidfran is one of those killed, and the survivors return to Wales, bringing with them the head of Bendigeidfran. Back in Anglesey Branwen dies of a broken heart. This is how this is described:

> And they came to the land of Aber Alaw in Talebolion. And then they sat down and rested them. Then she looked on Ireland and the Island of the Mighty what she might see of them. 'Alas, Son of God,' said she, 'woe is me that ever I was born; two good islands have been laid waste because of me!' And she heaved a great sigh, and with that broke her heart. And a four-sided grave was made for her, and she was buried there on the banks of the Alaw.

It may seem a bit churlish to point out the inconsistencies in this moving story. For instance, says Mac Cana, Efnisien's anger

49

at being ignored implies he knew nothing of the proposed wedding, yet he is said to have accompanied Bendigeidfran and Manawydan when Matholwch first announces his errand. But then there are many other inconsistencies in the *Pedair Cainc* which one has to forgive.

In the Third Branch, called Manawydan Son of Llŷr, Pryderi gives Rhiannon, his mother, in marriage to Manawydan, brother of Branwen. Fortunately they both like each other at once.

But one day an enchantment is cast over the whole of Dyfed, and houses, people and animals disappear. Part of the enchantment is that Manawydan and Pryderi, together with their wives, Rhiannon and Cigfa, are forced to seek their living in England where they spend their time making saddles, shields and shoes. So good are they at this that they are eventually driven out by the other craftsmen.

Eventually they return to Wales, but the enchantment is still at work, and this time Pryderi and Rhiannon are lost, leaving only Manawydan and Cigfa (Pryderi's wife). Manawydan finds a horde of mice devouring his wheat and manages to capture one. It turns out that this mouse is, in fact, the wife of the magician, Llwyd, son of Cil Coed, and he it was who was responsible for the enchantment on Dyfed, carried out in order to avenge the wrong done to his friend, Gwawl, at the bridal feast of Pwyll and Rhiannon. Manawydan now bargains with Llwyd. He tells him he will only release his wife if the magician lifts the enchantment and releases Pryderi and Rhiannon.

At last Pryderi and Rhiannon are restored and the country recovers its former state. Mac Cana suggests that the author of the Four Branches has created in Manawydan a reflection of his own personality and a vehicle for his own philosophy of life. He is the pragmatist and the peacemaker—he is cast as the protagonist of reason and enlightenment.

The Fourth Branch tells of Math, son of Mathonwy, who has a strange peculiarlity. It is that he can only remain alive as long as his feet are kept in the lap of a virgin, except when he is engaged in war. His present foot-holder is called Goewin but, unfortunately, his nephew, Gilfaethwy, falls in love with her and plots with his brother, Gwydion, to get her away.

50

Gwydion, who is also a magician, says he has the answer. He plans to bring about a war between the soldiers of Gwynedd, Powys and Deheubarth, the idea being that Math would then be fully occupied, so leaving the way clear for Gilfaethwy to have Goewin. Gwydion goes to Math and tells him about some marvellous swine owned by Pryderi, those that had come from Annwn, and promises to procure them for Math. He then tricks Pryderi into exchanging his swine for stallions and hounds, without telling him that they last for only one day. When the deception is discovered, it leads to a war between Dyfed and Gwynedd.

While Math is away, Gilfaethwy seizes the opportunity to burst into Math's bedroom, forcing the maidens out and raping Goewin. When the tearful Goewin tells Math what has happened he punishes the two brothers by changing them into animals. This punishment, however, only lasts three years and the three men are then reconciled. In the meantime Pryderi has been killed in the war. It is not related what happened next to Goewin but, of course, being no longer a virgin, she couldn't continue to be Math's foot-bearer.

So Math now takes Arianrhod, Gwydion's sister, as his new foot-bearer. But when Arianrhod is required to step over the wand to test her maidenhood, she fails dismally. She drops a yellow-haired boy child who is later named 'Dylan Eil Ton', Son of the Wave. The story-teller then says that she also drops something else:

> She made for the door, and thereupon dropped a small something, and before anyone could get a second glimpse of it, Gwydion had taken it and wrapped a silken sheet around it, and hid it.

He then rears the second child in secret and, when he grows a little older, Gwydion takes him to his mother at Caer Arianrhod. She is furious and swears the boy will never have name nor bear arms nor have a wife. But Gwydion succeeds by magic in securing all three for him. His name is to be Lleu Llaw Gyffes and his wife will be made of flowers:

> And then they [i.e. Math and Gwydion] took the flowers of the oak, and the flowers of the broom, and the flowers of the meadowsweet, and from those they called forth the very fairest and best endowed

51

maiden that mortal ever saw, and baptised her with the baptism they used at that time, and named her Blodeuwedd.

The story continues with Blodeuwedd being unfaithful to Lleu and plotting with her lover, Gronw Bebr, to kill her husband. But instead of dying, Lleu turns into an eagle and is discovered by his uncle, Gwydion, who breaks the spell. Then Gronw Bebr is killed and Blodeuwedd is changed into an owl.

This is the story turned by Saunders Lewis into one of the century's best plays, *Blodeuwedd*.

So these are the Four Branches. In the words of Professors Gwyn and Thomas Jones, the author 'created a miniature masterpiece. He achieved the effect of illumination and extension of time and space which lies beyond the reach of all save the world's greatest writers'.

Dr Thomas Parry has agreed that the stories themselves are often inconsistent, but the author shapes his sentences and puts them together in such a way as to produce a lively, rapid style. The narrative is liberally broken up with dialogue, which matches perfectly the mood and character of the speakers.

This is particularly true of the last *cainc*, in the scene where Blodeuwedd tries to find out from Lleu how he might be killed, so that she can pass the secret on to her lover, Gronw Bebr:

> And that night he [Lleu] came home. They spent the day in talk and song and carousal. And that night they went to sleep together, and he spoke to her, and a second time, but meantime not a word did he get from her.
>
> 'What has befallen thee?' he asked, 'and art thou well?'
>
> 'I am thinking,' said she, 'that which thou wouldst not think concerning me. That is,' she said, 'I am troubled about thy death, if thou were to go sooner than I.'
>
> 'Ah,' said he, 'God repay thee for thy loving care. But unless God slay me, it is not easy to slay me.'
>
> 'Wilt thou then, for God's sake and mine, tell me how thou might be slain? For my memory is a surer safeguard than thine.'
>
> 'I will, gladly,' said he.

Lleu then discloses the secret and the narrative continues.

No sooner had she heard this statement than she sent it to Gronw Bebr.

The scene throughout the Four Branches is forever changing, cause and effect follow each other rapidly and some of the dramatic moments are brilliant if frightening. There is one scene where Efnisien throws Branwen's child, Gwern, his own nephew, into the flames of the cauldron, a scene adapted chillingly in a recent modern television play inspired by the old story.

There is, however, a distinct difference between the controlled, disciplined style of the author of the Four Branches and the colour and ebullience of the other seven tales.

Culhwch and Olwen is probably the earliest of the tales. It uses the format of the familiar international folk-tale where the hero sets out to gain the hand of the daughter of a king or giant who then imposes a number of impossible tasks on all suitors, and, when they inevitably fail, he has them put to death. Culhwch and Olwen begins with a jealous stepmother who wants Culhwch to marry her daughter and, when he refuses, she swears that he will never lie with a woman until he wins Olwen, daughter of Ysbaddaden Chief Giant. The story of the tasks is then unfolded with exuberance and brings in characters from Arthur's court who come to the aid of Culhwch.

Lludd and Llefelys tells of three oppressions which afflicted Britain during the reign of Lludd. First the Coraniaid, whose hearing and knowledge were such that nothing could be said throughout the land without their knowing it. Secondly, a scream that was heard every May-eve which left women and animals barren and men without vigour. Thirdly, a mighty man of magic power who caused everyone to fall asleep and carried off all the food and drink from the king's courts.

In the Dream of Macsen Wledig, Macsen, emperor of Rome, was abroad hunting one day, when wearily he laid down to rest. In a dream he travelled to a far distant country, finally reaching a castle made of gold and precious stones. Inside sat a beautiful maiden dressed in rich silks. Just as the maiden, Elen, rose to greet him with a kiss, Macsen woke up, only to find that he had become obsessed with her. For a whole year his men had to travel the world in search of her, but in vain. So then Macsen was persuaded to re-enact the whole story of his dream, retracing his route—a process surely not unfamiliar to the modern psychiatrist—and, indeed, it worked for him, and all ended happily.

In another dream, The Dream of Rhonabwy, the eponymous hero, with two companions have been sent by Madog, ruler of Powys, to look for his brother, Iorwerth, who has gone raiding in England. The three manage to find lodgings in a very insalubrious house. That night Rhonabwy has a dream in which he reaches an island in the middle of the River Severn, upon which sits King Arthur. Proinsias Mac Cana suggests that this rumbustious tale is really a parody and, as such, is completely different from the other stories. The author, he says, keeps his tongue firmly in his cheek from beginning to end.

There remain the Three Romances—Geraint, Son of Erbin; The Lady of the Fountain; Peredur Son of Efrawg. Many scholars agree with Professor Bobi Jones's suggestion that these three were developed in a bilingual environment in Wales, most likely in the south-east in Glamorgan and the border areas, during the period after the Norman Conquest, and that the French influences in the Welsh texts were absorbed from the physical and cultural context of the time in Wales itself. They stress the protocol of knight errantry and courtly manners to a far greater degree than do the other stories.

There is obviously a lot more to be said about the Mabinogion. This is merely, I hope, an aperitif. We are fortunate in having good English translations. But, for readers of Welsh, who might find the original Old Welsh version a bit daunting, there is now an excellent modernised version by Dafydd and Rhiannon Ifans; and another, aimed at children, by Professor Gwyn Thomas. What Professor Thomas has to say in a note at the end for adult readers is particularly interesting. He admits that when he first began to prepare his children's version, his intention had been to tell the stories in his own words. But he soon discovered that this wasn't possible. All that remained were the bare bones of the stories. Somewhere in the process the true enchantment was missing. This, of course, is also true of any English translation however good it might otherwise be. He says:

When I realised this I began to see there was a profound truth in what is said of the old tales of India and Ireland and in the latter part of the Book of Revelations, which is, that no one should add to them nor take away. I came to feel that I would be betraying the tales by repeating them, without attempting to recreate the original wording.

The reason, I think, is that there is an element of ritualism in the original, and ritual speech depends on word-patterns and continuous rhythms. Ritual speech is similar to what is said about incantations, namely that the wording is all, and if that isn't got right, then the magic doesn't work. In getting too far away from the Mabinogi text, its very magic fades away.

It has been said that the Mabinogi contains traces of old Celtic gods and goddesses; that Rhiannon, Bendigeidfran and Lleu, for instance, are shadows of the old gods. There are certainly deeper implications in the story of Rhiannon on her steed in Arberth that reflect the old regions of our forefathers. That is why it is sacrilage to interfere too much with the original.

SOURCES AND FURTHER READING

The Mabinogion. Trans. Gwyn Jones and Thomas Jones. Everyman's Library, J. M. Dent.

Thomas Parry. *A History of Welsh Literature*. Trans. H. Idris Bell. Oxford University Press.

Glyn E. Jones, 'Early Prose: The Mabinogi', Chap. VIII in O.A.H. Jarman and Gwilym Rees Hughes. *A Guide to Welsh Literature*, Vol. I. Christopher Davies.

Proinsias Mac Cana. *The Mabinogi.* University Wales Press (Writers of Wales series).

— *The Mabinogi* (recent edition; Cardiff University Press).

THE POETS OF THE PRINCES

It was not only in the prose of the Mabinogion that remarkable work was being done at this time. After a long period of darkness, poetry as well as prose began to flourish from the eleventh to the thirteenth century. This was a time, you will remember, of the spread of Norman power. Gruffudd ap Llywelyn, Prince of Gwynedd, had been killed by treachery in 1063, and the land was broken up and divided between quarrelsome Welsh princelings. So the country was now ripe for Norman invasion. William the Conqueror himself had reached St David's, and his barons had established themselves both in north and south Wales. It looked as though Wales as a national entity was finished.

But in the year 1094 a great Welsh revolt broke out in north Wales, led by Gruffudd ap Cynan and Cadwgan ap Bleddyn. This spread rapidly towards the south and so successful was it that the Normans lost control of much of Wales. They were now largely confined to the south-east and to coastal lands of the south as far as Pembroke.

So now there was no stopping Welsh confidence and, for over a century, this resurgence was further fostered by lively and enterprising Welsh princes such as Owain Gwynedd, the Lord Rhys of Dinefwr and the two Llywelyns, who were able to postpone the final loss of Welsh independence.

There is usually an upside as well as a downside to turbulent times. The Norman invasions had obviously brought about tremendous changes in Wales, not least in the cultural life of the country. In addition to French influences, there was now much more travelling between Wales and Ireland. This was no doubt due to Prince Gruffudd ap Cynan. He had been born of a Norse-Irish mother and had been brought up in Dublin, but had returned to Wales, perhaps bringing with him Irish poets and musicians. Indeed, it is often said that he himself was directly responsible for introducing a number of important reforms in both poetry and music, although, once again, I have to add that this is now doubted.

But there is no doubt about these stirring national developments having been an important inspiration for the *Gogynfeirdd* —that strange name, which sounds even stranger in its English translation—the Fairly Early Poets. If you look back at the first chapter you will recall that the name was first used by Hengwrt antiquary, Robert Vaughan, in order to distinguish them from the *Cynfeirdd*, the early poets, such as Taliesin and Aneirin.

These later poets were attached to the courts of the independent Welsh princes. There was now, once more, a great sense of nationhood in Wales, with hitherto poorly organized kingdoms given renewed vigour. This spirit of independence reached its climax with the death of Henry I of England in 1135. To quote the historian, J.E. Lloyd:

> Everywhere the foreign yoke was cast off, the power of the new settlers dauntlessly challenged, and a new spirit of daring and independence seemed to have seized the whole Welsh race . . . Poets rising on the crest of the movement for independence transferred the passion of the people into song, and became the vanguard of a succession of Welsh poets which has continued to the present day.

In fact, at that time, that is, in the twelfth century, there was a Renaissance throughout western Europe. Abelard and Bernard of Clairvaux were at loggerheads with each other just at the same time as the first of these court poets, Meilyr Brydydd, was at the height of his powers. It was he, Meilyr, who composed an elegy to Gruffudd ap Cynan on that great chieftain's death in 1137, though perhaps best known is Meilyr's poem on his own death-bed.

These court poets were highly trained in their craft, their status being defined in the laws of Hywel Dda. The chief bard was called a *pencerdd* whose special chair in court was always placed next to the heir apparent.

Perhaps the most versatile of them all was Cynddelw, a forceful character, described by Saunders Lewis as a great master who controlled the poetic practices of the period. It is said (though this is questioned) that Cynddelw boasted in a contest with a fellow bard that he was known as a poet of learning and 'by virtue of my supreme diction, I am head of the chief bards'.

I should add that not all Cynddelw's poems, especially the love poems, are as self-promoting as that. Professor Joseph Clancy maintains that they reflect a way of life in which human relationships formed a complicated pattern, extending outwards through the family circle.

My own favourite poem of the period is the one by Prince Hywel, illegitimate son of Owain Gwynedd, called Gorhoffedd. The meaning of the word *gorhoffedd* is probably 'boast', but it also carries much of the force of the word 'exultation'.

But probably the best-known of them all today is the lament of Gruffudd ab yr Ynad Coch (Gruffudd son of the Red Judge) for Llywelyn the Last Prince, killed at Cilmeri near Builth in 1282. This is primarily a personal lament, but the poet expresses also the deep anguish of Llywelyn's people, and their sense of utter desolation in the face of a disaster they could only dimly begin to comprehend.

Saunders Lewis stresses the lyrical quality of the writing of this time, but J.E. Caerwyn Williams suggests that it is misleading to generalise about the *Gogynfeirdd*. Most of the poems are of an epic frame of mind, but many others have a

The memorial stone at Cilmeri commemorating the death of Llywelyn the Lasr Prince

distinctly religious spirit. In fact, says Professor Williams, their religious songs are far more numerous than their love songs. With few exceptions, we don't find outbursts of devotion, nor do they show understanding of the faith professed, but they are valuable because they preserve for us the Welsh layman's first attempts to express his Christianity in his native language.

GORHOFFEDD HYWEL ab OWAIN GWYNEDD (d. 1170)

Ton wen orewyn a orwlych bedd,
Gwyddfa Rhufawn Befr, ben teyrnedd . . .
Caraf ei morfa a'i mynyddoedd,
A'i chaer ger ei choed a'i chain diredd,
A dolydd ei dwfr a'i dyffrynnedd.
A'i gwylain gwynion a'i gwymp wragedd . . .
Caraf y morfa ym Meirionnydd,
Man y'm bu fraich wen yn obennydd.
Caraf yr eos wyrios wydd,
Yng Nghymer deuddyfr, dyffryn iolydd.

A foaming white wave drenches the grave,
The tomb of Rhufawn Bebr, chief of rulers . . .
I love its sea-strand and its mountains,
And the fort by the trees and its fair lands.
And its watered meadows and valleys,
And its white seagulls and lovely women . . .
I love the sea marsh in Meirionnydd,
Where a white arm was my pillow.
I love the nightingale on the privet
In Cymer of two rivers in the revered valley.

(Trans. Joseph P. Clancy)

59

GRUFFUDD AB YR YNAD COCH (fl. 1280)

MARWNAD LLYWELYN ap GRUFFUDD

Oerfelawg calon dan fron o fraw
Rhewydd fal crinwydd y sy'n crinaw.
Poni welwch chwi hynt y gwynt a'r glaw?
Poni welwch chwi'r deri'n ymdaraw?
Poni welwch chwi'r môr ym merwinaw'r tir?
Poni welwch chwi'r gwir yn ymgyweiriaw?
Poni welwch chwi'r haul yn hwyliaw'r awyr?
Poni welwch chwi'r syr wedi syrthiaw?
Poni chredwch i Dduw, ddyniadon ynfyd?
Poni welwch chwi'r byd wedi'r bydiaw?
Och hyd atad Dduw, na ddaw môr dros dir!
Pa beth y'n gedir i ohiriaw?

LAMENT FOR LLYWELYN ap GRUFFUDD

The heart's gone cold, under a breast of fear;
Lust shrivels like dried brushwood.
See you not the way of the wind and the rain?
See you not oak trees buffet together?
See you not the sea stinging the land?
See you not truth in travail?
See you not the sun hurtling through the sky,
And that the stars are fallen?
Do you not believe God, demented mortals?
Do you not see the whole world's danger?
Why, O my God, does the sea not cover the land?
Why are we left to linger?

(Trans. Anthony Conran)

SOURCES AND FURTHER READING

Ceri W. Lewis, 'The Courts Poets', Chap. VI in A.O.H. Jarman and Gwilym Rees Hughes. *A Guide to Welsh Literature*, Vol. II. Christopher Davies.

Anthony Conran. Introduction to *The Penguin Book of Welsh Verse, and translations.*

Joseph P. Clancy. *The Earliest Welsh Poetry.* Macmillan.

J. E. Caerwyn Williams. *The Poets of the Welsh Princes.* University of Wales Press.

THE POET OF SUMMER

Dafydd ap Gwilym considered generally to be Wales's greatest poet, was probably born sometime between 1315 and 1325. He was a member of a noble family which had by that time been for several generations on the side of the English king. His father was called Gwilym Gam, though, more than that, little is known of him, nor of Dafydd's mother, except that it was probably on her side that he was related to the uncle who had the greatest influence on his life.

This uncle, Llywelyn, was constable at the castle of Newcastle

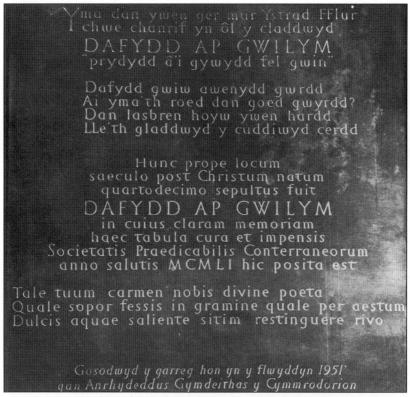

The Dafydd ap Gwilym memorial, Strata Florida

Emlyn, and is known to have sworn an oath of fealty to the Black Prince in 1343. One may wonder whether this was not an act of betrayal. But, no. To understand why not, let's look at the background of the times.

The sense of desolation following the death of Llywelyn in 1282 had given way to a kind of acceptance of the inevitable. The lands of the princes had been taken over by Edward I to be divided into counties, and castles sprang up to control the defeated Welsh. But if the princes had lost their power, there were others, many of the princes' former administrators, who seized the chance to clamber up the social ladder by giving allegiance to Edward.

In spite of all this, there was still a profound feeling of Welshness in the land, but, as A.D. Carr has pointed out, loyalties were personal rather than national now, and those who went over to Edward did not feel they were betraying their inheritance.

As we saw in the last chapter it was a time of great cultural development throughout Europe and these new ideas and influences seeped into Wales. There was still a sense of national identity but the new European atmosphere inevitably proved more stimulating than depressing for Welsh culture. (One wonders whether the same thing couldn't be happening today.)

So it was into this world that Dafydd ap Gwilym was born at Bro Gynin near Llanbadarn Fawr on the outskirts of Aberystwyth. His poems also show his connection with Newcastle Emlyn and the Teifi area. He died perhaps in 1360, though some suggest as late as 1380, and, like many others of the princes and nobles of Deheubarth, was buried at Strata Florida near Tregaron. However, some maintain that he was actually buried at Talyllychau Abbey near Llandeilo. Indeed, a memorial was erected to him in the churchyard there in 1984.

In her book in the Writers of Wales series, Rachel Bromwich describes vividly the world in which he moved. It was, she says, peopled with friars, nuns, pilgrims, hermits, tinkers, drovers, ostlers. In the country there were red deer and roebuck. Oxen were yoked in pairs for ploughing. Houses had glazed windows and lime-washed walls which might be gilded or painted with coats of arms. The poems show that Dafydd was familiar with sailing ships and parchment books and the signs of the zodiac with their influence on daily life.

A man with versatile interests obviously, and ripe to be the innovator that he became. In his poetry Dafydd had the confidence to use new language, metre and subject, which completely revolutionized the old bardic tradition without destroying its essentials. In his poems you will find elements of courtly love found in other European literature of the day, such as *Le Roman de la Rose*, and in the poetry of the Provençal troubadours. In this way Welsh poetry joined the mainstream of a wider tradition.

His uncle's important position as constable must have made him familiar with both English and French, and Dafydd obviously profited by this. In two early *awdlau* Dafydd praises Llywelyn's wide learning and culture, and describes him as a poet and linguist who 'knew all knowledge'. Not only was he Dafydd's bardic teacher, he was also in a position to have introduced his new nephew to literary influences far beyond the border of Wales.

So Dafydd was able to use French words which he now assimilated into his poetry, thus enriching his vocabulary, for he knew that these would be understood by his audience. He also made use of French lyrical forms such as the *pastourelle* and serenade.

But his *tour de force* was in the use he made of the *cywydd*. A *cywydd* is a poem in *cynghanedd* in seven-syllable rhyming couplets. In Dafydd's case these are normally between 30 and 60 lines in length, and it was in this form that he wrote his famous poems to nature and love. He hardly ever wrote one without reference to the other. For him the two were inextricable.

People have wondered about Dafydd's attitude to the religion of his age, and he has been pictured as an uncompromising enemy of monks, friars and the whole of the priesthood. But Thomas Parry maintains this is false. He was, he says, a true son of the Catholic Church but that doesn't prevent him from taking it as a theme for jesting. He compares the chants and liturgy of the church with the free life of the forests and the fields, always to the advantage of the latter. But it must not be forgotten that some of his verses had serious religious overtones, as in this poem to 'The Thrush':

> Music of a thrush, clear bright
> Lovable language of light,
> Heard I under a birch tree
> Yesterday, all grace and glee—
> Was ever so sweet a thing
> Fine-plaited as his whistling?
>
> Matins, he reads the lesson,
> A chasuble of plumage on.
> His cry from a grove, his bright shout
> Over countryside rings out,
> Hill prophet, maker of moods,
> Passion's bright bard of glenwoods.
>
> (Trans. Anthony Conran)

As Rachel Bromwich has said about his audacious use of religious imagery, 'The level of genuine devotion is assured in these poems as is that of supremely daring and provocative fantasy.' Indeed, it may have been these devotional verses that were the first to be transferred into the new medium of *cywydd*. His writing about nature is often linked to the wonder of God's creation.

The great advantage of his poems to us today is that they are among the first that can be reasonably understood by readers who know nothing of early Welsh. Translating them into English is a more difficult problem, and this could explain why Dafydd isn't better known outside Wales. It's acknowledged that doing adequate justice to his *cywyddau* in translation is an impossible task. Were it not for this, said W.J. Gruffydd, Dafydd ap Gwilym would rank among the greatest poets of medieval times.

The difficulties are pin-pointed by Rachel Bromwich:

> Any attempt to translate his poetry must take into account the complex requirements of *cynghanedd* as well as the depth of meaning which may underlie his use of particular words and phrases. By intricate innuendo and sometimes intentional ambiguities, with complex play on varied nuances of his traditional vocabularly and

of new words of French origin, Dafydd evolved for himself a poetic degree of complexity never previously envisaged in Welsh . . . The fact that poetry is untranslatable was never more true than in the case of Dafydd ap Gwilym.

It is interesting to speculate on the reasons why Dafydd left Dyfed to go to south-east Wales, but it was probably soon after his uncle's death that he took to wandering, following the tradition of the troubadours. We don't know when his first association with Ifor Hael (Ifor the Generous) began, but this was the man who welcomed Dafydd to his court in Glamorgan and became his friend and patron. In one of the poems he compares the privileges he enjoys in Ifor's home with those experienced by Taliesin in the court of Urien Rheged.

In one poem Dafydd described himself as a *gŵr â chorun* (a man with a tonsure) which suggests that he had qualified at some time for minor religious orders, apparently not an uncommon procedure at the time for those wishing to acquire education. He described himself in a number of passages as a member of the *clêr*, the *clerici vagrantes* or wandering scholars or troubadours. He was obviously influenced, albeit indirectly, by the erotic poetry of the Provençal troubadours. But the word *clêr* could also just mean poet in its older meaning. He certainly described himself as 'Bardd Ofydd', the poet of Ovid, recognised in the Middle Ages as the Poet of Love.

These wanderings throughout Wales were very productive for Dafydd, as he became familiar with streets and taverns and warehouses in places like Caernarfon, Aberystwyth and Bangor. These became settings for his more riotous poems of sexual adventure.

For instance, 'Trouble at a Tavern' recounts his adventures at an inn, where he lavishly entertains a girl with food and wine. Later that night he tries to enter her room but on the way his leg gets caught noisily in a stool. Then he bangs his head on a table and overturns it, together with the basin and copper pan upon it. The uproar wakes three sleeping English tinkers, Hickin, Jenkin and Jack, who immediately conclude their wares are being stolen. There is a great hue and cry and, in the confusion, the poet escapes safely into the darkness beyond.

The story is told swiftly, as befits a good anecdote. One can just imagine the fun Dafydd had in reciting it to his old friends. This is a farce at its best. But there's another aspect to it, and I should like to quote Anthony Conran's words in his introduction to *The Penguin Book of Welsh Verse*:

> If you read it merely as a romp you are in danger of ignoring Dafydd ap Gwilym. Dafydd came of a family that is known to have befriended the Anglo-Norman cause . . . Dafydd's playing at being a fine young aristocrat at a tavern in a town, was, therefore, an Anglo-Norman kind of behaviour; and his irony is on himself playing the Englishman, right from the start. This gives point to his using the phrase 'May Welshmen love me!' as a sort of swearword when he knocks his shin on the (English) ostler's stool. And at the very peak of his misadventure, with all hell let loose around him, he comes upon three Englishmen:
>
> > In foul bed, at the wall,
> > Bothered for their packs, and fearful,
> > Three English lay in panic—
> > Hickin and Jenkin and Jack.
>
> It is surely a judgment on him that the first thing they splutter is 'It's a Welshman!' and therefore a thief after their belongings. No wonder the poet exclaims 'O hot ferment of betrayal!' In fact, read properly, the poem is hardly contemptuous about the English at all. There is, I suppose, a certain snobbery in it; but this again is shot through and through with ironic undertones. After all, if Dafydd will try and make dates in the middle of the night in a crowded inn, and then gets caught in the act, he cannot expect to be treated as a visiting celebrity!

In another famous poem, 'The Girls of Llanbadarn', Dafydd describes how his attention is distracted during Sunday Mass at Llanbadarn church, when he overhears whispered comments on his personal appearance between two girls in the congregation.

His self-satire and tendency to exaggerate the effect his loves had on him were not acceptable to some of the more conservative poets of the time, who accused him of insincerity, if not of outright lying. The Anglesey poet, Gruffudd Gryg, for instance, challenged him in bardic contest about the hyperbole of his praises, saying that the glibness with which he threatened to die for any girl he serenaded made one wonder how the poor man had not already died twenty times already. Dafydd countered this by accusing Gruffudd of lacking originality.

But it was in the countryside he knew so well, especially in the forest, that Dafydd found the greatest inspiration for his poems. Certainly it was where he loved to meet his girls. As Geraint Gruffudd said in a lecture delivered at the National Eisteddfod at Aberystwyth in 1992, Dafydd rarely described nature purely, without there being some element of love as its counterpart. In spite of his amazing ability to identify with the natural world, he would use nature as a platform to express earthly love.

The poem 'The Magpie's Counsel' begins with a beautiful description of early spring, but then has the bird reproving the poet for his love of women and advising him to become a hermit (see page 74). In another poem he uses allegories from nature to describe his love. There are those, he says, who try to tame wild creatures, like the hare, the squirrel and the roebuck. However much these creatures are pampered, they always escape to their native haunts. The poet has tended his lady since she was eighteen years old, but lost her in the end.

Then again, just as birds nest under leaves, so love nests in the poet's heart. His breast was ploughed in January, sorrow sprouted there through the three months of spring. He made a fence around the crop on May Day, expecting a rich harvest, but he looked at Morfudd, and such showers of tears fell from his eyes that the crop was ruined.

Yes, Morfudd. The name of one of the two women who have stolen his heart. The other is Dyddgu. He calls Morfudd his favourite love and, as he himself proclaimed, he had composed 'seven and seven score' *cywyddau* to her (though nothing like this number has survived). He writes bitterly about the 'Bwa Bach' who became Morfudd's husband. It seems, says Rachel Bromwich, that behind his many allusions to her elusiveness and tantalizing treatment of him, it is likely that there lies a genuine story of deep and passionate love, ending in bitter frustration through her marriage to his rival.

It's true that Ifor Williams has tried to prove that these two women, Morfudd and Dyddgu, were imaginary, used as a means to express the poet's feelings about women in general. But more recent scholars, particularly D.J. Bowen and Eurys I. Rowlands, don't agree. They have both made out a convincing case for Morfudd having lived originally at Eithinfynydd, a farmstead still in existence between Llanuwchllyn and Dolgellau; moreover that she was related to the noble Nannau family, and that, although she lived at Llanbadarn after her marriage, she later died at Bryn-y-Llin, Abergeirw.

The two girls, Morfudd and Dyddgu, are portrayed as being completely different from one another. Dyddgu is sweet, good, wise and calm, above all, a lady of dignity, a dark, aristocratic and unattainable beauty. Dafydd knows she will always remain beyond his reach.

Fair-haired Morfudd is loving, a 'red ember', but married. She, too, is of high birth but, unlike Dyddgu, she has welcomed the poet with open arms. He responds gladly:

> Goris clust goreuwas clod
> Gorthoch—ni wnaf ei gwrthod;
> Lliw'r calch yn lle eiry cylchyn,
> Llyna rodd da ar wddf dyn.

> I did not refuse the collar which bound me,
> The poet's peer, for her arms around me
> Were white as the chalk or a circlet of snow
> How good the gift of man's throat will know.

But she is also inconstant and devious. She has deceived him many times, as carelessly as a ploughman changes a pair of oxen. In addition she is married to a jealous husband—the Bwa Bach (the Little Hunchback). When she got married, Dafydd swore he would never see her again, but that was a vow that kept on being broken.

His poems are full of the obstacles he keeps meeting in his pursuit of love. Something or other always seems to come between him and the woman he loves. The river Dyfi prevents him crossing on his way to Llanbadarn where his mistress awaits him. He can't kiss her because of a window which separates them. When he is really enjoying himself with his lady under the tree, along comes someone, noisily shaking a rattle, and this frightens the girl so much she runs away.

But it's the lady herself who worries him most. She's fickle, now welcoming him, now rejecting him. Or she's indifferent, caring nothing for the pain eating away at his heart. But the greatest obstacle of all is the lady's husband, the Bwa Bach. He watches over her continually and won't allow him near his love. But Dafydd assures her that even that won't prevent him finding a way to meet her.

What sort of people did Dafydd write for? D.J. Bowen says he always had a cultivated audience in mind, even in his 'simpler' poems, but that his popularity inevitably spread to the lower strata of society as well. As time went on he experimented with a simpler style, which bridged the gap between the formal poetry of the princes and later poets like Dafydd ab Edmwnd. This process, says Professor Bowen, could be seen also in the work of Chaucer.

So what do we make of Dafydd ap Gwilym? Iolo Goch, a contemporary poet, called him 'the jewel of the shires' and 'the hawk of women of the Deheubarth'. In an elegy on the death of his fellow-poet he wrote:

> Learning was immense in him,
> and he was tailor of love to a girl,
> and the harp of a court and its retinue
> and treasurer of minstrels and their praise
>
> and trident of battle and conflict,
> and pitiful without mitigation
> and presumption was the destruction of the man,
> and the beam of poets, most sorrowful is the world,
> and he will not rise up again;
> a strong, bold, sharp, clear-voiced teacher
> and lord was he, he went to heaven.
>
> (Trans. Dafydd Johnston)

Anthony Conran has called him the Charlie Chaplin of his time:

> His is decidedly the art of the great comic; like Falstaff he is not merely witty himself, but a great cause of wit in others, the girls

who mock him at Llanbadarn are as much part of his self-portraiture as his agonized reflections on them. And, like all great comics, he can be profoundly sad.

Geraint Gruffydd described how life to him must have appeared full of promise and joy at the start but the passing years had revealed the world as a devious place, and life a complexity of achievements and frustrations, with frustrations winning in the end. Though he rejected the Priest's accusations that his love for Morfudd was wholly sinful, he did acknowledge that there must have been a certan misbehaviour in their relationship, and in what purports to be his last poem he begs for forgiveness of the Trinity and the Virgin Mary. Dafydd was always conscious of God's presence, while being sceptical of the Church's teaching on morality.

But I'm going to let Sir Thomas Parry have the last word in what is, after all, a mere glimpse of Dafydd ap Gwilym:

> The never-ending wonder in his work is this. However overwhelming his poetic energy—the ideas bubbling up in his head, the images jostling with one another for expression, every sinew strained to the utmost in order to portray the exceeding splendours of his mistress—he never loses grip on his art nor does he forget the shape and pattern of the poem . . . Welsh literature has never seen a better poet than him.

TROUBLE AT A TAVERN

I came to a choice city
With my fine squire behind me.
At gay cost I ordered food
(Proud I had been from childhood)
At a worthy enough hostel—
Liberally; and wine as well.

I spied a slim fair maiden
(My sweet spirit!) at that inn.
On that bright-as-dawn sweetheart
Soon I'd wholly set my heart.
A roast—not to boast!—and costly
Wine I bought for her and me.
Youth loves good cheer. I called her
(How shy she was!) to dinner,
And whispered—I dared the trick,
That's certain—two words of magic.
I made—love wasn't idle—
Tryst to come to the spry girl
As soon as all our muster
Slept; black the brows she'd on her.

When at last, wretched journey!
All did sleep, save her and me,
I to reach the lady's bed
Most skilfully attempted.
But I fell, noised it abroad,
Tumbled brutally forward.
It's easier to be clumsy,
Rising from such griefs, than spry!

Nor was my leap unhurtful:
On a stupid and loud stool,
Ostler's work, to the chagrin
Of my leg, I barked my shin;
Came up a sorry story,
And struck—may Welshmen love me!
Too great desire is evil,
Every step unlucky still!—

By blows in mad bout betrayed,
On a table-top my forehead,
Where, all the time, a pitcher
And a loud brass cauldron were.
Collapse of that stout table—
Two trestles downed—stools as well
Cry that the cauldron uttered
Behind me, for miles was heard;
Pitcher shouted my folly,
And the dogs barked around me.
In a foul bed, at the wall,
Bothered for their packs, and fearful,
Three English lay in panic—
Hickin and Jenkin and Jack.
The young one spluttered a curse
And hissed forth to the others:

'There's a Welshman on the prowl!'
O hot ferment of betrayal—
'He'll rob us if we let him!
Look out you're not a victim!'

The ostler roused all the rest—
My plight was of the direst!
All round me they were angry
And searched for me all round me.
I stood in the foul havoc
Of rage, silent in the dark;
Prayed in no reckless fashion,
Hiding like a frightened man:
And such power has prayer for us,
Such the true grace of Jesus,
I found my own bed safe and sure
Though without sleep or treasure,
Thank the saints, freed of distress.
I ask now God's forgiveness.

(Trans. Anthony Conran)

THE MAGPIE'S COUNSEL

The magpie said—an indictment of (my) anguish—
proud, sharp-beaked upon the thorn-bush:
'Great is thy fuss, a vain and bitter chant,
Old man, all by thyself;
It were better for thee, by Mary, garrulous of speech,
beside the fire, you old grey man,
rather than here, amid the dew and rain
in the greenwood, in a chilly shower . . .'
'As for you, black-beaked Magpie,
hellish, very savage bird . . .
your nest is like a gorse-bush,
a thick creel of withered sticks.
You have speckled black plumage, precious, perfect,
your looks are ugly, and you have a raven's head,
motley-hued, with ugly home and raucous voice,
and every sort of far-fetched forceful speech,
you have learned, black speckled wing.

(Trans. Rachel Bromwich)

THE LADIES OF LLANBADARN

Plague take the women here—
I'm bent down with desire,
Yet not a single one
I've trysted with, or won,
Little girl, wife or crone,
Not one sweet wench of my own!

What mischief is it, or spite,
That damns me in their sight?
What harm to a fine-browed maid
To have me in deep glade?
No shame for her 'twould be
In a lair of leaves to see me . . .

74

In Llanbadarn every Sunday
Was I, and (judge who may),
Towards chaste girls I faced,
My nape to a God rightly chaste,
And through my plumes gazed long
At that religious throng.
One gay, bright girl says on
To t'other prudent—prospering one—

'That pale and flirt-faced lad
With hair from his sister's head—
Adulterous must be the gaze
Of a fellow with such ways.'
'Is he that sort?' demands
The girl on her right hand,
'Be damned to him, he'll stay
Unanswered till Judgement Day!'

O sudden and mean reward
For dazed love the bright girl's word!
Needs I must pack my gear,
Put paid to dreams and fear,
And manfully set out
Hermit, like rogue or lout.
But O, my glass doth show
With backward-looking woe
I'm finished, I'm too late,
Wry-necked, without a mate!

(Trans. Anthony Conran)

SOURCES AND SOME FURTHER READING

Thomas Parry. *A History of Welsh Literature*. Trans. H. Idris Bell. Oxford University Press.

Rachel Bromwich. *Dafydd ap Gwilym*   University of Wales Press (Writers of Wales series).

A.O.H. Jarman and Gwilym Rees Hughes. *A Guide to Welsh Literature*, Vol. II. Christopher Davies.

Anthony Conran. *The Penguin Book of Welsh Verse*.

Meic Stephens and Gwilym Rees Hughes. *Poetry Wales*, Special Dafydd ap Gwilym Number, Spring 1973.

Joseph P. Clancy. *Medieval Welsh Lyrics*. Macmillan.

THE POETRY OF THE UCHELWYR

One of the first things Edward I had done after the death of Llywelyn in 1282 was to turn the old Welsh provinces into shires, with the result that the whole social fabric of Wales seemed to change. Garrisons were planted throughout the country, and English settlers were encouraged to trade in places forbidden to the Welsh. But, however great the oppression, there are always natural survivors, and we have seen how some of the gentry prospered—people like Dafydd ap Gwilym's uncle Llywelyn, for instance, who, by compromising with the authorities, got himself special privileges.

But it was a different story for most of the population, those living outside the castle walls, who were no longer protected by their feudal lords, and who had to scrape what living they could in a hard, new world. In spite of their sufferings they must have found time to enjoy some sort of poetry, music and dance, but nothing has come down to us of the folk culture of that period. The bubonic plague, the Black Death of c. 1349, exacerbated their plight and left serious social problems in Wales. Moreover, the acquisition of free land by outsiders, encouraged by Edward, led to a further erosion of tenants' rights, and there was an increased growth of a class of landless labourers. Little wonder, then, that small bands of outlaws took to hiding in the vast forests, getting what they could by pillaging and killing.

Here were all the ingredients of explosion, and explode it did in 1400 with the revolt of Owain Glyn Dŵr. Owain himself was a descendant of the royal house of Powys, and was lord of Glyndyfrdwy in Meirionnydd. He was also descended through his mother from the royal house of Deheubarth at Dinefwr. This made him a natural leader for the inevitable uprising. It was a vicious war, but Wales, under Owain's magnetic leadership, fought with a new found vigour, fired by the belief in the old prophecies that the millenium would usher in an exciting new age for Wales.

Tradition has it that Owain Glyn Dŵr was crowned Prince of Wales at Machynlleth in 1404 in the presence of emissaries from France, Spain and Scotland. Two years later, at Pennal in Meirionnydd, he made a treaty with Charles VI of France in which, in return for a transfer of religious allegiance in Wales from Rome to Avignon, he demanded recognition of an independent Welsh church and the establishment of two universities, one in north and one in south Wales. Obviously this was not going to be recognised in England.

The end became inevitable when Owain mysteriously disappeared. The bubble burst and almost immediately whole communities made their peace with Henry V. Later poets had little to say about their late leader, perhaps because they assumed he was dead, perhaps because after all the suffering that war brings, they just wanted to forget. Even the poet, Iolo Goch, who had written the famous *cywydd* to Owain's court in Sycharth doesn't refer to the revolt. A tragic ending indeed to a brave struggle.

Owain Glyn Dŵr
The statue by Alfred Turner, stands in City Hall, Cardiff

But, as far as Welsh literature is concerned, a new age was now born. Those in high places were anxious to give their patronage to writers and musicians, for the new landed proprietors were all out to impress each other. Between the years 1300 and 1600 a vast quantity of literature of high order was produced. This was the period of the poetry of the *uchelwyr*. These were gentry who were glad to welcome the bards into their homes. The bards in their turn were glad to be able to travel from hall to hall as they were invited. Among them was Iolo Goch who wrote poems to families in Gwynedd and his own home in the Vale of Clwyd. But he did write about other parts of Wales as well. A well-known *cywydd* of his depicts a dispute between soul and body, with the soul recounting its journey from place to place, naming, among other places, Newtown, Builth, Blaenau Taf, Kidwelly, Ystrad Tywi and Strata Florida. He was probably the first poet to make use of the *cywydd* to sing the praises of his patrons. His Sycharth poem, already mentioned (see page 81), gives a graphic description of life in the great houses of the time.

In a small book like this I can do no more than list some of the other poets—Lewis Glyn Cothi, Dafydd Llwyd of Mathafarn, Dafydd Nanmor, Dafydd ab Edmwnd, Guto'r Glyn, Tudur Aled and the great bardic teacher, Gruffydd Hiraethog.

But I should like to mention one poet in particular, and that because, unusually, she was a woman. You may have noticed a dearth of women's names, though there are lots of Anons! Not much is known about Gwerful Mechain, apart from the fact that she came from Mechain in Powys. One of her *cywyddau* indicates that she was an innkeeper, who used to join in bardic contests with the men. A fellow poet called Ieuan Dyfi wrote a poem attacking women's perfidy throughout the ages, and this was sharply answered by Gwerful. Perhaps it was in order to prove herself the equal of the male poets that some of her poems were decidedly erotic. But it is generally agreed that her best work was religious, particularly her fine *cywydd* to the sufferings of Christ.

Her well-known *cywydd* 'Cartref Gwerful' (see page 84) begins with the hope that someone will provide her with a harp. With it she will entertain the men who come to her hostelry with silver. The price of a dinner is two pence. (Could this have been the first ever tourist advert?)

The poems of this period depicted a society which believed in good living, feasting and carousing. They give us a picture of generous hospitality on the part of patrons, of groaning tables and of fine wines from Gascony and Poitou. This, of course, is a reflection of the growing network of medieval trade throughout the known world, with spices from India and exotic new furnishings for the houses. Not everyone approved. The poet Siôn Cent wrote disapprovingly of their fine houses, kitchens, cellars, horses, hounds and cattle, and their trips to England.

But obviously all this enhanced the prestige of the poets. For centuries they had formed themselves into a kind of guild and it wasn't easy to break into their circle. Occasionally during the fifteen and sixteenth centuries they used to hold conferences in different parts of Wales to lay down rules of their craft. These were called *eisteddfodau* (very different from the ones we know today, of course). They included competitions, as they do today, but the serious business was to consider the purely technical aspects of their work. One of the first of these was held at Caerwys near Mold in 1523, which might be considered to be the first National Eisteddfod of all. In it two famous bards, Gruffydd ab Ieuan and Tudur Aled set out rules for the awarding of degrees, having had authority to do so by commission from no less a person than Henry VIII.

IOLO GOCH (*c.* 1320-98)

LLYS OWAIN YN SYCHARTH*

Addewais yt hyn ddwywaith,
Addewid teg, addaw taith . . .
Myned, mau uned ddain,
Lles yw, tua llys Owain.

Fo all fy naf uchaf ach,
Aur ben cler, dderbyn cleiriach,
Clywed bod, nis cel awen,
Ddiwarth hwyl, yn dda wrth hen,
I'w lys ar ddyfrys ydd af,
O'r deucant odidocaf,
Llys barwn, lle syberwyd,
Lle daw beirdd aml, lle da byd.
Gwawr Bowys fawr, beues Faig,
Gofuned gwiw ofynaig . . .

A gwraig orau o'r gwragedd,
Gwyn 'y myd o'i gwin a'i medd!
Merch eglur llin marchoglyw,
Urddol hael o reiol ryw,
A'i blant a ddeuant bob ddau,
Nythaid teg o benaethau.

Anfynych iawn fu yno
Weled na chlicied na chlo,
Na phorthoriaeth ni wnaeth neb,
Ni bydd eisiau budd oseb,
Na gwall, na newyn, na gwarth
Na syched fyth yn Sycharth . . .

*Selections only. The translation overleaf is not line for line but slightly fuller than the above, though not complete.

THE COURT OF OWAIN GLYN DŴR
AT SYCHARTH

Twice have I promised you this
A journey of fair promise.
A man should not be backward
If he can keep his word . . .

My lord of lineage sovran
Can well receive an old man.
Poets make common knowledge
He delights to gratify age.
To his court I hurry ahead
Most splendid of two hundred.
Court of a baron, courteous home
Where many a poet's welcome.
Lo, the form of it—a gold cirque
Of water held by earthwork;
A court with one gate and bridge
Where a hundred packs have passage.
There are rafters coupled there
Joined two and two together.
It's French, this Patrick's belfry,
Westminster cloister, easy of key . . .

The roof's tiled on each gable
There's a chimney that draws well.
Nine halls in true proportion
And nine wardrobes in each one.
Elegant shops, comely inside,
And stocked as full as Cheapside,
A church cross, lovely limewhite,
Chapels and the windows bright,
Each part full, each house in the court,
Orchard, vineyard and whitefort . . .

A fine mill on strong water
A stone dovecot on a tower,
A fishpond walled and private
Into which you cast your net,
And, no question of it, bring
To land fine pike and whiting,

A lawn with birds for food on,
Peacocks and sprightly heron,
Servants to get each job done
Supplying all the region,
Bringing best Shrewsbury beer,
Bragget and choice liquor.
Poets from everywhere gather
Every day together there.
The best wife among women,
I'm blest by her mead and wine,
Daughter from knights descended,
Noble, generous, royally bred.
And his children come in pairs,
A fine nestful of rulers.

Lock or latch very seldom
Has been seen about this home.
No one need act as gateman,
Here are gifts for every one—
No hunger, disgrace or dearth,
Or ever thirst in Sycharth!

(Trans. by Anthony Conran)

GWERFUL MECHAIN (fl. 1462-1500)

CARTREF GWERFUL

Cynnal arfer y Fferi
Tafarn ddi-farn, ydd wyf fi;
Cryswen loer, croesawa'n lân
Y gŵr a ddaw ag arian.
Mynnwn fod, wrth gydfod gwŷr
Fyd diwall i'm lleteuwyr.
A chanu'n lân gyfannedd
Yn eu mysg wrth lenwi medd.

I keep the custom of the Ferry, a tavern none can fault; a white-robed moon gives sweet welcome to the man who comes with silver. My desire is to satisfy, to make a perfect world for my guests, to sing among them in this lovely home as I pour out the mead.

EIRA

Eira gwyn ar fryn oer fry—a'm dallodd
    A'm dillad yn gwlychu.
Myn Duw gwyn, nid oedd genny
Obaith y down byth i dŷ.

White snow on a cold hill has blinded me, and my clothes are wet through. By the blessed God, I lost all hope I should ever get home.

SOME SOURCES AND FURTHER READING

A.O.H. Jarman and Gwilym Rees Hughes. *A Guide to Welsh Literature,* Vol. II. Christopher Davies.

Dafydd Johnston. *Iolo Goch: Poems.* Gomer.

Dafydd Johnston. *Medieval Welsh Erotic Poetry.* Tafol.

J. E. Caerwyn Williams. *The Poets of the Princes.* University of Wales Press (Writers of Wales series).

THE BIBLE AND THE HUMANISTS

But then came change and the tradition of elaborate poetry declined. The accepted reason for this was the Act of Union of 1536, which attracted the gentry away from Wales to England, —the Cecils and the Salisburys and the Middletons, for instance —where they eventually became Englishmen. Not all, however. It was during this time that gentry like Robert Vaughan, of Hengwrt, Dolgellau, became immersed in the old Welsh manuscripts. Vaughan did Wales immeasurable service in preserving and copying out these works, which could otherwise have been lost forever.

It was in 1546 that the very first book in the Welsh language was printed. It was called *Yn y lhyvyr hwn* (In This Book). The author was Sir Siôn Prys, a gentleman of Brecon, who was married to a niece of Thomas Cromwell. Up to this time all books which had reached Wales had been either in English, Latin or Greek. This, of course, coincided with the Renaissance in Europe with its emphasis on the classics and religious works. Prys's aim was to see these books printed in Welsh. This was soon followed by William Salesbury's translation of parts of the Bible into Welsh.

In 1563, that is, in Elizabeth's time, a law was passed ordering that the Bible and Book of Common Prayer be translated into Welsh, and William Salesbury was summoned to undertake the task with Richard Davies, Bishop of St David's, and Thomas Huet, his precentor. Although Salesbury's translation of the New Testament was generally considered a fine piece of work, he had used some rather idiosyncratic spelling, which cut across the orthographic tradition of the language of the poets. Twenty years later the whole Bible was magnificently translated by Bishop William Morgan in 1588, and this was the Bible we all knew until the new version was launched in 1988.

One of William Morgan's chief assistants was Dr John Davies, rector of Mallwyd, near Machynlleth, for over 40 years. It was probably he who was responsible for the revised translation

Frontispiece of William Morgan's translation of the Bible

of the Morgan Bible and of the Book of Common Prayer. He was regarded by his contemporaries as an outstanding scholar in many fields, including Greek and Hebrew. His Welsh Grammar and Dictionary are among the greatest glories of the period. In it Latin is placed alongside Welsh and its preface is wholly in Latin. Other prose writers such as Morris Kyffin and Rowland Vaughan, Caergai, Llanuwchllyn, translated important English religious works.

An eighteenth-century portrait of William Morgan

But poetry itself was not dead. Edmwnd Prys, a relative of William Salesbury, sought new forms of free verse which could be accessible to the common people. This was much frowned upon by the traditionalists, but Prys's answer was that you could not successfully turn the psalms into *cynghanedd*, though he himself did use a little in his own adaptations.

> Disgwyliaf o'r mynyddoedd draw
> Lle daw im help wyllysgar
> Yr Arglwydd rhydd im gymorth gref
> Hwn a wnaeth nef a daear.

—which is a rendering of the psalm 'I will lift up mine eyes unto the hills'. This measure was subsequently adopted by Vicar Prichard of Llandovery who used it and others like it for popular verse with a moral message, as in his condemnation of the people of Llandovery:

> Mene tecel, tre Llanddyfri
> Gwelodd Duw di yn dy fryntni.

(Mene tecel, town of Llandovery, God has seen thee in thy squalor.)

The term, humanist, used here is quite different from the one we use today, which generally is another name for atheist or agnostic. Humanism in Renaissance times was based on a reverence for the classics, following the thought of Aristotle in literature and the authority of reason. However, it was Cicero in particular who was the prose model of these classicists.

The movement had begun with the discovery of classical manuscripts. These were published and translated and formed the basis of the new learning. The classics were, of course, pagan writings and, as such, influenced contemporary culture, and this inevitably led to a counter revolution publishing books on Christian doctrine. In the meantime there developed a kind of snobbery against the use of the indigenous language. Latin or Greek was everything. In France, Joachim du Bellay urged his fellow countrymen to turn their backs on French forms and to model their writings on classical Latin and Greek writers. Even Milton in his earlier years wrote in Latin until he eventually returned to writing in English. This debate between the rival claims of Latin and the mother tongue spread throughout Europe and had its effects in Wales, though the rediscovery of the Welsh classics meant that Welsh humanists better appreciated the glories of their own language.

In his book in the Writers of Wales series, Ceri Davies describes how, in the summer of 1590, Dr Siôn Dafydd Rhys dedicated the manuscript of his Grammar of the Welsh Language to Sir Edward Stradling of St Donat's Castle in Glamorgan. The grammar was written in Latin, at the behest of his patron whose wish was 'that the Welsh language might be more easily spread to other nations too'. And, of course, Latin was the only language in which to communicate with the international readership of Renaissance Europe. After studying at Oxford, where he had his first contact with sixteenth-century thought and learning, Rhys had gone to the University of Siena in Italy where he had graduated as a Doctor of Medicine.

With the persecution of Catholics in the reign of Elizabeth certain other Welsh scholars had chosen to flee the country and settle in Italy, more than one of them coming to hold responsible offices in the Roman Church. The renewed interest in Greek and Latin classics, says Dr Davies, had inspired these Welsh humanists to search for the manuscripts of their own country and to assert that Wales had a literature which would stand comparison with the noblest of Greek and Latin works. Some of these expatriates published books in Welsh using the printing presses of France and Italy, and, considering their distance from Wales, their achievements were remarkable.

Morys Clynnog had been appointed Bishop of Bangor, but Elizabeth came to the throne before he could be consecrated, and, being a Catholic, he was forced to flee the country, so he returned to Louvain where he had previously studied law. His friend, Gruffydd Robert, had also left for the Continent in 1559, and they spent two years together at Louvain before settling in Rome in 1564. Three years later Gruffydd Robert moved to Milan, as confessor to Carlo Borromeo, Archbishop of Milan, and it is as Gruffydd Robert of Milan that this fine scholar is best known.

Gruffydd Robert was concerned about what he thought was the poverty of contemporary Welsh literature, which he considered to have declined after the Act of Union. He came to the conclusion that the Welsh must be re-taught their grammar. The first part of his Grammar was published in Milan in 1567 and the rest probably after the death of Borromeo in 1584. This was very well received and even admired back home by Protestants such as Morris Kyffin, who wrote:

> I have seen a brief handbook to the first part of a Welsh Grammar printed some time ago which is part of a learned work on the grammatical art, so pure, so smooth, so excellent in style, that it is not possible to desire anything more perfect in this respect.

The main thing to decide, according to Gruffydd Robert, was what sort of language the literary Welsh should be. He considered the language used by the bardic tradition to be too formal and conservative. The poets of this tradition refused to write in contemporary Welsh. One reason was that their instruction was always in secret, so they obviously didn't want their craft to become too popular. Gruffydd Robert taught that the use of language was an art to be learned. The only purpose of the old bards in their writing was to preserve the old forms of the language so that it wasn't contaminated by English, but that led to distancing themselves from the living language. Gruffydd Robert maintained that the language used by the people should be respected and cultivated.

Morris Kyffin was also critical of the contemporary Welsh poets. He accused them of having little learning: 'What is needful to the Welsh tongue is learning and godliness, not letters to set forth learning.' He said that to translate the Bible into Welsh would put learning into the language, and he was proved right as it turned out, for that is exactly what happened. But although humanists and traditional poets differed so much, they both loved their country and their language and were critical of those who had turned their backs on their heritage. Gruffydd Robert wrote:

> You will find some men, that, as soon as they see the River Severn, and hear the Englishman but once say good morrow, they shall begin to put their Welsh out of mind and to speak it in most corrupt fashion. Their Welsh will be of an English cut, and their English (God knows) too much after the Welsh fashion. And this cometh either with very foolishness or a saucy pride and vanity. For he is never seen for a kindly, virtuous man that will deny whether it be his father, or his mother, or his country, or his tongue.

Saunders Lewis said that Gruffydd Robert was the father of modern Welsh writing. The ideas of these men made a great difference to the quality of Welsh prose at a very critical time. To them language was something to be delighted in, to be handled and turned over and fondled, to be loved apart from its content.

SOURCES AND FURTHER READING

Ceri Davies. *Latin Writers of the Renaissance*. University of Wales Press (Writers of Wales series).

THE SEVENTEENTH CENTURY

From a literary point of view the seventeenth century is generally considered to have been a gloomy period in Wales. It wasn't that there was a scarcity of poets but they lacked the learning or mental vigour to invent new methods, or so said Dr Thomas Parry. Poetry had become less and less attractive to the well-born and educated, many of whom had become anglicised. What was left became more and more of a medium of amusement or moralizing for the uninstructed masses. True that for a time there were still a few household bards attached to the gentry, but these gradually vanished. One of the last of the 'paid' bards was Siôn Dafydd Las of Llanuwchllyn, who was bard at the house of Nannau near Dolgellau.

Perhaps this accounted for the growing enthusiasm at that time for copying and preserving the works of the very early Welsh poets, for that sort of activity usually flourishes at a time when old things are passing away. Of course this wasn't confined to Wales alone. An antiquarian movement was in vogue in England at the same time, a movement with which Robert Vaughan of Hengwrt, Dolgellau, was associated. But in Wales, without these antiquaries, many of whom were neither poets nor writers, the whole output of the early poets would have perished.

Robert Vaughan (1592-1667) had gone to Oriel College, Oxford, in 1612, but had left without a degree. He married the daughter of Gruffydd Nannau and settled at Hengwrt. His main interest lay in the history of Wales, and this is what led him to the old manuscripts. He copied the Black Book of Carmarthen in facsimile and collected the manuscripts of the White Book of Rhydderch and the books of Taliesin and Aneirin. A couple of centuries later his library was sold to W.R.M. Wynne of Peniarth, Llanegryn, and is now part of the National Library of Wales.

All this is not to say there were no poets during the century. There were bright spots such as the love poems of Edward

Hengwrt, Dolgellau, the home of Robert Vaughan

Morris of Perthillwydion, near Cerrigydrudion, and the carols of Huw Morus of the Vale of Ceiriog (page 100). There were also folk poems, *hen benillion*, reflecting the lives of the common people at various times of the year, with wassail songs and carols at Christmas, in the New Year, for May Day and at harvest time. There were harp stanzas (*penillion telyn*), though we don't know the names of the authors. Probably most of them had been handed down from generation to generation. The atmosphere is mainly rural, bounded by the seasons, depicting the weather, love, courting, death and sorrow; a pagan life to a great degree, with depths of longing and heartfelt sadness, and yet plenty of sly humour.

The verses are quite simple, and appear to be effortless (but you just try composing one!). In their simplicity lies their strength. Anthony Conran suggests that they were probably not popular with the gentry because those people had their own special kind of love poetry, that of the *cywydd* writers. It is certainly a pity this simpler kind of verse was not further developed in order to produce in Welsh poetry something to take the place of the old tradition. Apparently no one realised its true value before Lewis Morris in the following century, although Richard White, Rhys Prichard and Morgan Llwyd

92

borrowed the metre and simple diction to proclaim religious truths. Perhaps one could say that the same thing is happening in Wales today when the 'true value' of some of our modern pop songs is beginning to be taken seriously.

So, in the seventeenth century, there were three kinds of poetry—the old strict verse, the carol verses and the *penillion telyn*. For the greater part it was the poetry of the unlettered. In a country which possessed neither a university nor a cultural centre, the period from 1650 till the middle of the nineteenth century is merely one unbroken effort to give the Welsh sufficient education to enable them to understand religious teaching. Poetry had to struggle on as best it could.

Prose, on the other hand, flourished. This happened because learned gentlemen and clerics like Rowland Vaughan, Morris Kyffin and John Davies, set about translating English religious classics into accessible Welsh. The main aim of these men was to proclaim the need for godliness among their countrymen rather than the employment of elegant language and literary adornment. Their style was pure and dignified but, as Dr Thomas Parry says, the misfortune of these classics is that their matter is so devoid of interest to us today they are hardly ever read.

The exception is the work of the Puritan, Morgan Llwyd. He wrote clear but vigorous prose, which can give great enjoyment to us even today.

It is interesting to compare the seventeenth century with our own. The turmoil and unrest following political upheaval and tremendous scientific discoveries are certainly not unknown to us today. First of all Galileo proved that Copernicus had been right in asserting that the planets, including the earth, revolved around the sun, instead of the other way about. Then William Harvey discovered how blood circulated, revolutionising medicine; and Isaac Newton showed how the universe was regulated by simple mathematical laws. All of which greatly upset previously held religious beliefs.

It was a century which had rejected the old feudal ways of thinking. For the first time ordinary men and women felt free to think for themselves. But what usually happens then is that while one man feels strongly on one issue, his neighbour may

93

feel as strongly on the opposite side, and this inevitably leads to clashes and ultimately to violence. The Civil War was a culmination of all this ferment. The Church of England considered itself to be a powerful defender of the existing social and political order, with Charles I keeping a firm hold on what was said from the pulpit. But the new class of people, hungry for freedom of thought and knowledge, rebelled against this control and found its expression in Puritanism.

Morgan Llwyd was born in 1619 in Cynfal Fawr, Maentwrog. His father died when he was young and his mother took the fifteen year old boy to Wrexham to be educated, probably to prepare him for either holy orders or law. Wrexham, being so close to the English border, had become an important centre for Puritanism in Wales and, while still a schoolboy, Morgan Llwyd was greatly affected by the preaching of the Puritan, Walter Cradock, who had settled briefly in Wrexham. Cradock, who was obviously an uncompromising preacher, had so angered

Cynfal Fawr, Maentwrog, birthplace of Morgan Llwyd

local brewers by his castigation of strong drink, that they had banded together to force him out of town. When he left Wrexham for Llanfair Waterdine in Shropshire, Morgan Llwyd joined him there, later following him to Llanfaches in Monmouthshire, where the first Congregationalist church was established in 1639. During his three year stay there Llwyd met and married Ann Herbert, and they had eleven children. He tells the story of his life in a poem called 'Hanes Rhyw Gymro' (The Story of a Welshman). A shortened version with translation is on page 103-4.

On the outbreak of the Civil War Morgan Llwyd sent his wife and children to his mother in Cynfal and then joined the Parliamentary Army as chaplain. In 1644 he was sent by the Parliamentarians to north Wales as a travelling preacher, eventually settling once again in Wrexham, at a place called Brynffynnon rented to him by his friend, the Regicide Col. John Jones, Maesygarnedd. His work during the years 1650-53 was as one of the Approvers under the Act for the Propagation of the Gospel in Wales. This meant being responsible for finding suitable ministers to take the place of those who had lost their livings.

In one respect he was quite different from the other Welsh Puritans, and that was in his love for Wales and in his ability to write in Welsh. He was among the first to write books in Welsh as distinct from the translations. His language patterns were not those of his scholarly classical predecessors like Gruffydd Robert, nor really of the Bible, though that was his sustenance, but he used the colourful speech of the people of his Meirionnydd home. *Llyfr y Tri Aderyn* (The Book of the Three Birds) is considered today to be one of the chief classics of the Welsh language. It takes the form of a conversation between three birds:

a) The Eagle (that is, the Parliamentary government and its administration, and probably Cromwell). It is the Eagle who puts the questions to the other two birds, and in some degree holds up the balance between them.
b) The Raven, who represents the Crown and the established episcopal church, is probably to be identified with the Cavaliers.

The raven has a rough, cruel voice, boasting about her cunning. She believes in law and order and fears that the Puritan sects aim to turn society upside down.

c) The Dove, who possesses the truth. The dove represents the Puritans, whose religion is not bound by institutions, but who follow the vision given them by God.

You can read more about Morgan Llwyd in a book by M. Wynn Thomas in the Writers of Wales series. In it he suggests that, unlike his more militant contemporaries, Vavasor Powell and Thomas Harrison, Llwyd sought to create a spiritual revolution in men's hearts, rather than through political upheaval. Most of the Puritans based their doctrines on the epistles of Paul, and Morgan Llwyd was no exception to this, but he was just as much influenced by the mystical imagery of Jacob Boehme, a German philosopher.

Another movement which influenced his thought was that of the Fifth Monarchists. Like many others at the time, Llwyd believed that the Second Coming of Christ was nigh. This reached its climax during the 1640s with this strange sect, who believed that the four empires—Assyria, Persia, Greece and Rome—had already come to an end, and that a new one was dawning when Christ would come to reign in person. From the Book of Daniel they reckoned this would happen some time in the years either 1650, 1660 or 1666.

This is how W. J. Gruffydd defines Boehme's philosophy:

It is in the believer himself that Christ's sacrifice takes place, it is not a thing that happened once to set right something which had previously happened in Eden. In other words Eden and Calvary are not in time. Secondly, heaven and hell are states not places; they too are not in time. Thirdly, the laws of nature are the laws of God, and they cannot be changed or frustrated by a miracle, or in any other way, and hence all creation moves to some final salvation, but not in time or in this world.

M. Wynn Thomas has shown intriguingly in another book, *Morgan Llwyd: Ei Gyfeillion a'i Gyfnod*, how one of Boehme's favourite characters was the Virgin Sophia, that is, the wisdom of God. For Boehme, Sophia was even more important than the

96

Trinity. In fact, for him she was one of a four-part Godhead. Morgan Llwyd did not go as far as this but he did adapt Boehme's beliefs about Sophia in his own writings. This is Boehme's explanation of the Fall of Man:

> When Adam was first created, his spiritual partner was Sophia. But Adam closed his eyes to Paradise. He fell asleep and was lost in dreams in which Sophia had no part. Instead, he found a new companion, Eve, and she was the first indication that he had fallen into a human, physical, sensuous world.

All somewhat esoteric, perhaps, so we turn with relief to the other influence on Morgan Llwyd, namely that of the Quakers.

In the early days of Quakerism, Llwyd had sent two messengers to George Fox to find out more about his beliefs. What he learnt certainly influenced his own writings, particularly the belief in the voice of conscience as distinct from the voice of the church or Bible or anything else external which might determine man's behaviour.

'There is a light burning within which can show the way.'

Many of Morgan Llwyd's followers joined the Quakers because he himself had already proclaimed a message so similar to theirs. But he was critical of the fanaticism of some of those early Quakers. When his mother wanted to know his attitude to this new sect he told her: 'They tell the truth, but not the whole truth, and we know that there must be water as well as fire in the spirit.' In any case, from April until Christmas 1653 he was convinced that the Parliament of Saints would succeed in preparing the country for the Second Coming. It was no time to be joining a new sect. And of course one does not forget that he had been appointed by the government to be an officer for the Propagation of the Gospel in Wales.

When Cromwell unceremoniously ended the Parliament of Saints in December 1653, the hopes of radicals like Morgan Llwyd were shattered. That was when for a short time he joined the Fifth Monarchists. But by 1656 he was claiming publicly that Cromwell's authority should be respected. Yet he continued to defend the Quakers and to recognise that the mystic qualities of their beliefs were close to his heart.

As to his writing, there is no doubting the rhythm and beauty of his prose. Dr Gwyn Thomas has said that the work of all the seventeenth-century writers was meant to be read aloud. Poetry, especially *cynghanedd*, had always been intended for the ear rather than the eye, but the prose writers of this century were mainly preachers. They didn't seek to entertain but to teach, to show people how to live in this world in preparation for the next. Morgan Llwyd's great achievement was that he combined both entertainment and spiritual teaching in his fine prose.

EDWARD MORRIS (1607-1689)

GYRRU'R HAF AT EI GARIAD

Mae'r wlad yn dy hoffi, mae'r blodau'n dy hoywi,
  Mae Fflora'n dy gwmni da heini dy hun;
A thithau mor enwog, a'th siaced wyrdd wlithog
  Ariannog fotymog, fyd twymyn.

Mae'r coedydd yn glasu, mae'r meillion o'th ddeutu,
  Mae dail y briallu yn tyfu ymhob twyn,
A'r adar diniwed yn lleisio cyn fwyned
  I'w clywed a'u gweled mewn gwiwlwyn.

SENDING THE SUMMER TO HIS LOVE

The whole world doth love thee, the flowers doth light thee,
  And Flora's thy friend in this frolicsome play,
And thou in thy dewey green jacket so pretty
  With buttons of silver in May.

The woodlands are greening, the clover's around thee,
  The leaves of the primrose beginning to move,
And innocent blackbirds now trilling so sweetly
  Can be heard, can be seen, in the grove.

HUW MORUS (1622-1709)

MOLAWD MERCH

Fy nghalon i sydd
Yn danfon bob dydd
At flodau brig dansi lon ffansi, lawn ffydd;
Mor bêr yw dy bryd
Fel rhos ar lan rhyd,
Yn loyw wen lili neu deg bwysi'r byd;
Dy gusan di-gêl
Yw'r mwsg ar y mêl,
Cnewyllyn dy ddeufin i'm dilyn y dêl;
Mwy braint a mwy bri
Cael ymwasgu â thydi,
Na chyweth brenhinieth, gwen eneth, gen i.

Nid ydyw da'r byd
A'i hyder o hyd,
I wŷr ac i wragedd, ond gwagedd i gyd;
Mawr serch a hir sai'
Da drysor di-drai,
Yn hwy o flynyddoedd na thiroedd na thai;
Cei draserch heb droi
A chalon i'w chloi
Os wyt ti, f'anwylyd, yn dwedyd y doi;
Os tynni di'n groes
Mae'n berygl am f'oes!
O gariad, dwys drawiad, madawiad nid oes.

100

PRAISE OF A GIRL

My heart every day
Doth speed on its way
Glad fancy to tansy top, faithful and gay;
As sweet is your pose
As a river-bank rose
Or a posy where lily or lavender blows;
Like honey musk is
Your unconcealed kiss,
The kernel of your lips I cannot dismiss;
There's more state and fame
In clasping your frame
Than if I'd the wealth of a king to my name.

The goods of the earth
And trusting their worth
To men and to women are all void and dearth;
Great love maketh sure
A wealth will endure
Where houses and lands vanish ages before.
Much love will you see,
And my heart and its key,
My dear, if you say you will come with me;
But if you draw back
'Tis a perilous lack—
My life is so wounded, there's no return track.

(Trans. Anthony Conran)

101

HIRAETH

Dwedwch, fawrion o wybodaeth
O ba beth y gwnaethpwyd hiraeth?
A pha ddefnydd a roed ynddo
Na ddarfyddo wrth ei wisgo?

Derfydd aur a derfydd arian.
Derfydd melfed, derfydd sidan,
Derfydd pob dilledyn helaeth,
Eto er hyn ni dderfydd hiraeth.

Hiraeth cas a hiraeth creulon,
Hiraeth sydd yn torri 'nghalon.
Pan wyf dryma'r nos yn cysgu
Fe ddaw hiraeth ac a'm deffry.

Hiraeth, hiraeth, cilia, cilia,
Paid â phwyso mor drwm arna'
Nesa tipyn at yr erchwyn,
Gad i mi gael cysgu ronyn.

Tell me, oh you great in wisdom
Tell me now what is this yearning?
Of what fine stuff is it woven?
That it never fades with wearing.

There's an end to gold and silver,
Silk and velvet all doth vanish.
Every cloth must fray and crumble
But no lesser grows my *hiraeth*.

Oh, so cruel and oh so hateful,
Through my tears my heart is breaking.
When at night my dreams are deepest
Hiraeth comes to give me wakening.

Hiraeth, hiraeth, stop tormenting,
Stop your pressing on my heartache.
Move away from this thy bedside,
Let me sleep before the morning.

MORGAN LLWYD (1619-59)

HANES RHYW GYMRO

Ym Meirionnydd gynt y'm ganwyd,
Yn Sir Ddinbych y'm newidiwyd,
Yn Sir y Mwythig mi wasnaethais,
Yn Sir Fynwy mi briodais.

Ym Morgannwg cenais heddiw,
Drannoeth neidio i Sir Gaerloyw,
Yng Ngwlad yr Haf mi gefais aeaf,
Gwelais Fristow deg yn drymglaf.

Sir Ham i'r dierth a wnaeth groeso,
Wrth Gaer Peris cas orffwyso,
Yn Nhref Llundain wedi disgyn,
Rhaid rhoi'r bywyd mewn rhyw blisgyn.

Gwynt yng Nghent, a rhaid yw hwylio
Ar draws y moroedd i Sir Benfro,
Drwy'r tân drain, oddi yno ymaith
I waelodion Lloegr eilwaith.

Drwy'r dymhestloedd eto i Gymru,
Yn nhref Baldwyn ennyd llechu,
Ac oddi yno i Wrecsam decaf,
Pa ddyn a ŵyr ple'r eiff o nesaf?

Ond mae'r camrau wedi'u mesur,
Cyflog, gwaith, a'r nerth i'w wneuthur,
Ym mhob tref roedd rhyw anniddos,
Ond roedd E' 'mhob lle'n ymddangos.

Nid yw oes y byd ond wythnos,
A'r mawr Sabbath sydd yn agos,
Paratowch cyn dyfod trigain,
Gwae'r Twrc, Cythrel, Cnawd a Rhufen.

A WELSHMAN'S STORY

In Merionnydd I was born,
In Denbighshire was changed,
In Shropshire I served,
In Monmouthshire I married.

In Glamorgan I sang today,
The next day in Gloucestershire,
Winter found me in Somerset,
I saw sadness in lovely Bristol.

Hampshire welcomed a stranger,
Porchester gave me rest.
In London Town where I landed
Life was put within a shell.

Wind in Kent then off to sail
Over the seas to Pembrokeshire,
Through a fire of brambles onwards
To the depths of England once more.

Through the storms once more to Wales,
Rest a while in Montgomery,
Then on to lovely Wrexham,
What man knows where he goes next?

But my footsteps were measured
Wage and work, and strength to do it.
Every town gave certain trouble,
But He appeared in every place.

A lifetime is but a week,
And the great Sabbath draws near.
Prepare, before the sixty arrives,
For woe to the Turk, Devil, Flesh and Rome.

Selections translated from *Llyfr y Tri Aderyn* (Morgan Llwyd)

Eagle: You talk of the shepherd. But there are many voices in the world, and the sounds of much arguing. How did you recognise the voice of the Holy Spirit amid all this?

Dove: Do you not know that a little lamb may recognise the voice of its mother among a hundred sheep? No one can fathom the true spirit but he who is naturally a part of it. And so it is vain to give signs and words in order to know it.

Eagle: By this you are entrusting everyone to his own thoughts.

Dove: When the true shepherd speaks, and man hears him, the heart burns within, and the flesh trembles, and the mind lights up like a candle, and the conscience reacts as wine in a bottle, and the will bends to the truth; and that strong small voice raises the dead from the grave to wear his crown and to change his whole life, to live like the lamb of God.

Eagle: What, according to you, is this flesh we speak of, since many do not understand their own words?

Dove: The flesh is everything under the sun which is outside the inner man. Whatsoever is transient and not eternal, that is flesh. Flesh is in the senses of man and pleasures of the world. Flesh is the play of old and young. Flesh is the food and heritage of man. Flesh is time and everything that passes. Flesh is the will and secret of men. Flesh is many prayers and preaching. Flesh is the honour of great men and of small men. Flesh is all that the natural man may see, hear, have and hold. And all flesh is straw . . . Woe, woe, to all who live in the flesh; they cannot please God, nor be saved, unless they return.

Extract from *Gwaedd yng Nghymru*
(A Cry in Wales)

Oh people of Wales! To you doth my voice come, Oh inhabitants of Gwynedd and Deheubarth, Unto you do I call. The dawn has broken, and the sun is rising upon you. The birds are singing: Awake, oh Welshman, awake. And if thou believe not words, believe deeds. Look about thee and see, behold the world and its pillars are shaking. The earth is in commotion. There are thunders and lightnings in the minds

105

of the peoples. Behold the hearts of many do tremble (though they confess it not) as they look for the things that are to come. The great day of the Lord searcheth and trieth every secret thought: And many seek a place to hide under their own leaves, and under the aprons of the old Adam: the wise men doubt, and the strong tremble. The speakers swallow their words, and the subtle bite their tongues. Dear friends accuse one another, and every man (well-nigh) is divided within himself, the great houses are split as under the small houses crack . . . the life and time of every man run like a weaver's shuttle, and the great world of eternity draweth nigh to all, and to thee also who readest or listenest to this. Therefore it is full time for thee to awake from thy sleep, and to seek for the strait path and to be acquainted with the truth, and to follow it heedfully.

Trans. H. Idris Bell

ELLIS WYNNE (1671-1734)

We are still in the seventeenth century, but only for a while. Our main writer here spans the end of the seventeenth and the first thirty-four years of the eighteenth century. He is known generally as 'Ellis Wynne o'r Lasynys'—Glasynys being a farm between Talsarnau and Harlech, not very far from the home of Morgan Llwyd in west Meirionnydd.

Details of his early schooling are vague. We do know, that in 1692 he went to Jesus College, Oxford, where he graduated, though exactly what his degrees were is not quite clear. There is a tradition that one of them was LL.B. If he had originally had his eye on becoming a lawyer, he must have become pretty disillusioned, for lawyers were among the chief targets of his abrasive wit.

In 1698 he married Lowri Wynne, who died in childbirth the following year. In 1702 he married another Lowri, of Hafod Lwyfog, Nant Gwynant. They had nine children, four of whom died young.

It was in 1703 that he published his best-known work, *Gw
eledigaethau Y Bardd Cwsc* (Visions of the Sleeping Bard). The following year he was ordained Deacon of the Church of England, and afterwards became rector of Llanbedr and Llandanwg. In 1611 he moved to Llanfair, near Harlech, as rector, and stayed there until his death in 1734.

Although he had translated some religious works into Welsh, it is the *Gweledigaethau* which has secured for him a lasting place in our literature. Actually it was based on Roger L'Estrange's English version of the work of the Spaniard Don Quevedo's *Visions of Hell* but, in spite of its involuted journey (Ellis Wynne called it 'in imitation of . . .'), the Welsh version became, in effect, a completely new work, reflecting what he himself saw in the immediate world around him.

Throughout the first half of the century, there had been a growing conviction that the end of the world was at hand—in fact, according to the Fifth Monarchists, it was to happen in 1666! But 1666 came and went, and the world was still in its place, though still full of wickedness. Although nothing had so far happened, there remained a preoccupation with eschatology, and an interest in the Other World. This was much reflected in seventeenth-century English literature, for instance, Tom Brown's *Letters from the Dead to the Living*; Milton's 'Paradise Lost'; Bunyan's *Pilgrim's Progress*. We ourselves are familiar today with a fascination with other planets, but, as Gwyn Thomas points out in the Writers of Wales series, in the seventeenth and eighteenth century the Other World was made into a dark mirror to reflect the wrongs of this world.

Ellis Wynne shows us the lower realm of Death and Hell. Among the targets of his satire are apothecaries, lawyers, sharpers, vain women, Catholics, Quakers and Cromwell. So there's hardly any need for me to add that he was strongly Royalist (Queen Anne, of course). He could be abusive, vigorously direct and often wrote in the crude speech of the largely monoglot common people around him. However, his underlying purpose was serious and based on sincere religious convictions.

This is what Saunders Lewis had to say of him:

108

Ellis Wynne's purpose in writing was didactic. His political and religious opinions were those of the Church of England of his day. He disliked both Nonconformists and 'Papists'. He placed Louis XIV and Cromwell together in his picture of Hell. His religion was that of the arid eighteenth-century morality untouched by 'enthusiasm'. The queen, champion of the English church, is the central figure in the house of God. Indeed, this writer, like many of his countrymen, was more English than the English.

The Visions begins with a first paragraph familiar by now to nearly all lovers of Welsh literature:

One fine afternoon of a warm, long yellow summer, I went my way to the top of one of the mountains of Wales, and with me I took a telescope to aid my weak eyes, to see the far-off near and little things large; through the thin, clear air and the splendid, quiet warmth, I espied far, far away, over the Irish Sea, many pleasant prospects. At last, having feasted my eyes on all kinds of pleasant-nesses about me, until the sun was about to reach its ramparts in the west, I lay down on the grass thinking how fair and how comely (compared to my own country) were the far-off lands of whose gentle plains I had caught a glimpse; and how splendid it would be to have a full view of them, and how content were those who had seen the course of the world compared with me and my like; thus by travelling far with my eyes and then with my mind, languor came, and in languor's train your Master Sleep came stealthily to tie me up; and with his leaden keys he locked the windows of my eyes and all my other senses safely tight.

Gwyn Thomas (all of whose translations these are) describes what happens next. In that sleep, the Bard is shown the course of the world by a shining angel. The world is set out as a City of Destruction with a number of streets on it. Belial rules this city of wide streets and towers, rules it through his daughters, Pride, Profit and Pleasure, and through Hypocrisy who holds court there.

The three streets run downwards to the gates of Belial's Enchanted Castle. A small but neat street crosses these three. It is on a higher plane and goes towards the City of Immanuel. The noise of a futile attack by Belial's forces is what wakes the Sleeping Bard at the end of this vision. There follows a poem about the great building of the world, once created perfect but spoiled by sin.

The second vision tells how one cold night the Sleeping Bard is approached by master Sleep and his sister Nightmare who are going to visit their brother Death. Nightmare soon departs in a huff, but Sleep takes the Bard with him to the other side of the City of Destruction. Here are the Rooms of Death, their doors open to the Land of Forgetfulness where Eternity begins. The Bard is led by Lucifer, Death's father, who exchanges letters with his son. The journey ends in a bottomless hollow near which Justice keeps court.

The third and last vision is the Vision of Hell. The Bard falls asleep somewhere near the Severn and is taken upwards by the angel through the Milky Way and Pleiades until the limits of Eternity are reached. There they behold two realms of Death, one on the right, one on the left. The Bard has already been through the left one and now wants to see the other, but permission is refused. Instead they go down into the chasm between the two:

> A vast country, very deep and dark, without form and without inhabitants, sometimes cold and sometimes hot, sometimes silent and sometimes noisy with torrents of waters falling on the fires and extinguishing them; presently you would see a blast of fire breaking out that would singe the water dry. So there was nothing orderly there, nothing whole, nothing alive, nothing elegant, nothing but an outstanding inconsistency and a dark astonishment.

The angel then leads the Bard through various cells and chambers in Hell where he is shown the tortures of the damned. Lucifer makes a speech to his parliament in Hell. This particular speech is reminiscent of Milton's Lucifer, but Wynne has made his Lucifer bombastic and also an inefficient, malevolent bungler. These elements come to the fore in a rebellion in Hell perpetrated by Papists and by Cromwell's followers. It shows excruciating chaos. Another parliament follows where sins in the form of devils present themselves as the most appropriate to subvert the blessed kingdom of Britain under its holy queen, Anne. The sin chosen for this task is Easy-Time. The vision ends with the Dante-esque figure of the giantess Sin and with hints of ultimate Hell which is beyond the power of words to describe.

The whole book concludes with a poem which tells how heavy the heart is with all the sights of Hell, but it encourages those who are still alive, still on this side of the wall of Eternity, to be of good cheer, for on this side there is still hope through Christ.

Of his style, one could say it is sometimes reminiscent of Swift, for instance in his use of paradox, when he takes us by surprise by giving a completely different angle from the one we've been led to expect. Like the whore who says:

> A thousand curses on my parents . . . for sending me to a nunnery to learn chastity; they would have done as well to have sent me to a Roundhead to learn to be generous, or to a Quaker to learn morality, as to send me to a Papist to learn how to be chaste.

Here is an impression of some ladies in the Street of Pleasure:

> . . . many a horned coquette like a ship in full sail parading as if in a frame with quite a junk shop about her, and from her ears a good farm's worth of pearls.

Or the Alderman:

> At this a long pole of a man who had been an Alderman and who had held many offices came out beneath us, spreading his wings as if to fly, and he—he could hardly shuffle from one foot to the other, on account of his belly and his gout and many other gentlemanly ailments.

Or the lover who practises his gestures:

> He was looking in a mirror learning to smile properly without showing his lady-love too much of his teeth.

Also the more sexually unpleasant passages such as this one:

> If this one's beauty has enticed you to lust for the woman's body, she [i.e. the Princess of Pleasure] has only to raise a finger to one of her father's officers (who are always about her though not seen) and they will straight away convey to you a woman, or a whore's

111

body newly buried, and they will go inside it, instead of a soul, lest you be frustrated in such a goodly purpose.

Here now is what another critic, Tecwyn Lloyd, has to say:

> He enjoyed mocking the strict, formal, classical writers by using everyday, sometimes coarse, idioms. He pretended to be uncultured and rough like some of his contemporaries whom he admired— L'Estrange and Ned Ward (who was put in the pillory for writing coarse verses about the Whigs) . . . What strikes one about the Visions is that they were travels, travel in the company of another person who knows his way around . . .

The search for happiness became an important theme in the eighteenth century, but for Ellis Wynne, the only place in which the Sleeping Bard could find real happiness was in his own place on this earth, that is, in the warm kitchen of Glyn Cywarch on a winter's evening with a good companion at the fireside. And he writes lyrically of 'fine April mornings with the Earth resplendent in a livery of leaves; fine houses, beautiful gardens, full orchards, shady meadows fit for secret meetings . . .' And yet these are the very things he castigates in his description of the Street of Pleasure. In fact, says Tecwyn Lloyd, Ellis Wynne in the Visions is two persons. On the one hand there is the artist who appreciates colour and form; on the other is the harsh moralist who hates all man-made art. As it happens, it is the artist who wins in the Visions. It is the remarkable style of the writing that has survived.

EXAMPLES OF STYLE

1. Presently twenty devils like Scotsmen with packs across their shoulders appeared and let them fall before the throne of despair, and, on enquiry, what they carried turned out to be Gypsies. 'Ha!' said Lucifer, 'how did you know other people's fortunes so well, without knowing that your own fortune was leading you to this place?' There was not a word of reply so astonished were they at seeing here things more odious than themselves. 'Throw them,' said the king, 'to the witches in the upper shit-house, because their faces are so like the colour of faeces. There are no cats here or reed candles for them, but let them have a frog among them every ten thousand years if they be quiet, and don't deafen us with their jingle-jangle-clang.'

2. And I don't have the words to set forth her attributes. But I can say that she is a three-faced giantess, one most pernicious face towards heaven, yelping, snarling and spewing abominable filth towards the heavenly king; another face set fair towards the earth, to entice men to remain in her shadow; and the other terrible face towards hell to torment it for ever and ever. She is greater than all the earth, and yet increases daily, and she is a hundred times more hideous than all hell; it is she who caused hell to be made, and it is she who fills it with inhabitants. If she were removed from hell, then the inferno would become paradise; and if she were removed from the earth, this little world would become heaven; and if she were allowed to go to heaven, she would turn bliss itself into Ultimate Hell. There is nothing in all the worlds (save her) that God did not create. She is the mother of the four deadly Enchantresses, she is the mother of Death and the mother of all evil and wretchedness; and she has an awesome grasp on all living men. She is called *Sin*.

(Trans. Gwyn Thomas)

SINGERS AND PLAYERS

Printing was now coming into its own. For centuries all the popular songs, ballads and carols, verses sung and spoken from one generation to another, had had to depend for their survival on folk memory, and it was inevitable that much was lost along the years. Verses in the strict metres of the old bardic tradition, fostered by the patronage of the gentry, had long been circulating in manuscript but, by the end of the seventeenth century, the printed works of Edmwnd Prys, Ficer Prichard and Morgan Llwyd, with their declared aim of appealing to the ordinary people, meant that poems in a simpler language had become more easily accessible.

By the end of the seventeenth century new printing presses had been opened in Shrewsbury, and later on they began to appear in Wales, particularly at Trefriw, Machynlleth, Carmarthen and Dolgellau. These presses would publish almanacs, chapbooks and pamphlets containing perhaps two or three poems to be sold by pedlars in markets and fairs around the country. Huw Jones of Llangwm, for instance, earned a living as a pedlar selling ballads he had published himself.

These poems appealed to the common man's fondness for an exciting story, tales of murder and shipwreck, of mistaken identity, earthquakes and epidemics. There were satirical poems about new customs like tea-drinking and women's fashions; about the wars against France and America; many religious poems with moral lessons; many love poems, some quite lewd.

Then there were the Interludes, a kind of versified drama acted on a wagon in a farmyard, or in the street at a market or fair, or even on a table in an inn kitchen. An Interlude originally meant a short play between two acts of a longer play. It later developed into an independent form, mostly in the northern counties of Wales, probably influenced by wandering players from over the English border. The actors were not professionals but young country workers who had played in what spare time they had after harvesting. Here is a verse from an Interlude in the year 1774:

Ni gawsom ddigon o lawenydd
Wrth golli amser eger ogwydd
Ffeind oedd chware, caru a rhodio
Ni ddaliwn ati flwyddyn eto . . .
Ni gawsom gywir barch a chariad
Drwy beder sir mewn difyr dyddiad,
Clyche yn seinio, canu a dawnsio
Yr hyn yn lwcus yr wy'n ei leicio . . .
Ni fuon wyth o bur gymdeithion
Efo'n gilydd yn un galon,
Deuddeg gwaith ar hugen heleth
Y darfu dangos hyn o'n chw'ryddiaeth . . .

We had lots of merry-making
While wasting time in eager talking
Twas good to play and love and travel,
We'll do it again another year . . .
We were appreciated and loved,
Entertaining throughout four counties.
Bells rang. There was singing and dancing.
Luckily tis what I like to do . . .
Eight true companions were we,
Together in one accord
Playing all of thirty-two times.

Then they would all return to their daily work:

Rhai at wair a rhai at fedi,
Rhai'n ddi-siarad at waith seiri.
Rhai bob tro at waith go' i'w gofio mewn gefel,
Pob amodau, pawb i ymadael.

Some to hay and some to reaping,
Some in silence back to woodwork.
Some to recall it all in the smithy,
All conditions, all must depart.

The plays were written by home-spun poets, usually in four-line stanzas. Chief among them was Twm o'r Nant (Thomas Edwards [1739-1810]) of Denbigh. He had begun early. In his autobiography he says:

115

Before I was twelve years old, seven boys from Nantglyn decided to act an Interlude, and they took me with them (something of which my parents had mixed feelings) to act the part of a girl. For I had the best singing voice in the neighbourhood.

Twm o'r Nant

There was always a fiddler in these plays, who would often break out into a jig. There were always two traditional characters, usually the Fool and the Miser. The other characters were up to the writer, and they would act out some story from political or social history. The Fool would dress up in what he called his 'livery', that is, a periwig, spotted jacket and hose with bells attached. Sometimes he would be carrying a staff, but nearly always a cudgel shaped like a phallus to shock the women in his audience.

The other character, the Miser, usually wore ragged clothes and a cap called *cap y cybydd*, the miser's cap, and the audience always looked forward to the arrival of Death who would come and take the Miser off stage to be buried in a grave. It was this Miser's Cap which Twm o'r Nant eventually threw into the River Conwy when he decided to stop 'following the Interlude', because, he said, he had fallen in love with a girl who was 'inclined to religion'. But before that happened he had created some memorable characters and written plays full of social criticism.

In *Tri Chydymaith Dyn* (The Three Companions of Man), *Cyfoeth a Thlodi* (Wealth and Poverty), *Cybydd-dod ac Oferedd* (Avarice and Dissipation), *Pleser a Gofid* (Pleasure and Care)—he constantly attacks idle priests and clergy lacking zeal, Methodists more intent on religious extravagances than honest living, the greed of stewards, and so on. The theme is presented

116

by various characters such as Captain Wealth, Lady Lusts of the Flesh, Reginald Money-Bags. The Miser complains of his lot, of the low price of farm produce, of crushing taxes, of the way his dissipated son spends all his money and of his wife's extravagance.

The players weren't popular everywhere. Elizabeth Baker of Dolgellau, writing in her diary, said, 'Tis amazing that, for a single penny for admittance of each person, these Buffoons get from 25s. to 30s. a night for two or three nights successively.' As the century progressed they increasingly drew on themselves the wrath of the Methodists and, by the end of the century, Interludes had vanished, scorned out of existence.

But there's no keeping a good poet quiet and the Interlude writers probably moved on to the *eisteddfodau*, whose followers met in taverns to discuss the old strict metres and to compete in improvising *englynion*. It is recorded that at their eisteddfod in Bala in 1738 a dozen poets were present composing various *englynion*—to the local gentry, to wine, to one another and to Bala itself.

SCHOLARS AND THE MORRIS CIRCLE

Elizabeth Baker, an Englishwoman who had come to live among the gentry of Meirionnydd, was, in spite of her lively diary, probably ignorant of the traditional interests of the people around her, particularly of their literature and history. She doesn't seem to have been aware of the work of scholars like the local antiquarians, nor of men like Edward Lhuyd, Keeper of the Ashmolean Museum at Oxford, and author of *Archaeologica Britannica*. This remarkable man was both a naturalist and a specialist in Celtic studies. The *Archaeologia*, published in 1707, contained a grammar of each of the Celtic languages. Unfortunately, he died before he could complete more than one volume of his great intended work.

But it was the scholarship of men like Lhuyd that made way for a group of cultural enthusiasts known as the Welsh Augustans (after the better known circle of Pope, Dryden, Swift, Addison and Steele). These were primarily the three Morris brothers—Lewis, Richard and William. They wrote long, lively letters to each other, full of opinions and probably prejudices on scholarship and literature, and, delightfully, on people.

Lewis Morris (1701-65)

Lewis and William both became customs officers, Richard a highly placed naval clerk in London and founder there of the Society of Cymmrodorion. A fourth brother, John, went to sea, and another John, a nephew, kept up the family tradition by writing letters full of colourful, sometimes lewd, descriptions. Bedwyr Lewis Jones called him the 'Boswell *Cymraeg*'.

Born in Llanfihangel Tre'r-beirdd, Anglesey, the eldest of the three, Lewis, liked to claim that his education had not been

Archæologia Britannica,

GIVING SOME ACCOUNT

Additional to what has been hitherto Publish'd,

OF THE

LANGUAGES, HISTORIES and CUSTOMS

Of the Original Inhabitants

OF

GREAT BRITAIN:

From Collections and Obfervations in Travels through
Wales, Cornwal, Bas-Bretagne, Ireland and *Scotland.*

By EDWARD LHUYD M.A. of *Jefus College,*
Keeper of the ASHMOLEAN MUSEUM in OXFORD.

VOL. I.
GLOSSOGRAPHY.

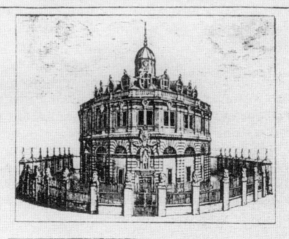

OXFORD,
Printed at the THEATER for the Author, MDCCVII.
And Sold by Mr. *Bateman* in *Pater-Nofter-Row, London* : and *Jeremiah Pepyat*
Bookfeller at *Dublin.*

'regular', though scholars today have disputed this. He was undoubtedly the ablest of the three. Poet, map-maker, botanist, surveyor and technician—these were only some of his accomplishments. His interests were remarkably wide, but his greatest love was for the history of Wales and its literature. He would pronounce judgement on the writings of his contemporaries with great insight and some acidity. His letters, written in a racy, muscular style, are a mine of information about the way the people of Anglesey and, later, Cardiganshire, lived at that time.§

There were other members besides the brothers, all influenced by the Queen Anne - George I period in English literature. This is how Saunders Lewis describes them in his 'A School of Welsh Augustans':

> The urbanity of the Morrisians is revealed in the unperturbed mode of life reflected in their works. They were Whigs in politics, loyal to the Hanoverian kings; England's enemies were theirs, and much of the sycophancy of nineteenth-century Welsh poetry may be traced to their influence.

The most prolific, and arguably the most gifted of the circle, was Goronwy Owen. Also an Anglesey man, he was born at Llanfair Mathafarn Eithaf in 1723. His mother, Siân Parry, had been a servant at the home of the Morris family. She was, however, no ordinary woman. Goronwy once said that he 'never knew a Mother, or even a Master, more careful to correct an uncouth, inelegant phrase or vicious pronunciation than her'. His father, a goldsmith, had been able to teach him the elements of *cynghanedd*, although he himself was no poet. Goronwy spent four years at Friars' School, Bangor, studying Classics with a view to becoming a parson. In 1742 he went to Oxford, but stayed there only one week, possibly because of lack of money, but it could have been because of his natural contrariness. There followed a period as assistant teacher at Pwllheli Grammar School, then at Denbigh Grammar School. Then in January 1746 he was ordained deacon at Bangor, and sent as Bishop's Chaplain to his native parish of Llanfair Mathafarn Eithaf as curate.

What happened next was a great disappointment which

changed his life. Many years later, in a letter to Richard Morris in 1752, he described what had happened. After he had been there for three happy weeks, he was told that a well-connected young man called John Ellis of Caernarfon had asked the Bishop for a curacy within his diocese. Goronwy, having neither wealth nor connections, had to go. The only place available to him was over the English border, near Oswestry.

This was not to be the answer to his troubles. He seemed to be unable to manage his practical affairs, to say nothing of his personal life, and books and poetry meant nothing to him now. As he said later in a letter to William Morris:

> Had I, when I liv'd in Oswestry, been as nice a critic in valuable old books as I was in voluble young women, I might have furnish'd myself pretty moderately; but who can put an old head upon young shoulders?

Then in August 1747 he married Elin, daughter of a prosperous merchant, so one would have thought his future now looked rosy. However, the following year he was imprisoned in Shrewsbury for debt and trespass, and was only freed by the generosity of a Shrewsbury draper. But all this forced him to move with his wife to nearby Donnington to be curate and schoolmaster. Here he began to find a certain peace, and he rediscovered his love of literature. As Branwen Jarvis says in her notable book in the Writers of Wales series:

> The two years spent at Donnington reveal another Goronwy, a man whose enthusiasm for literature had been rekindled, and who set about the tasks of gaining knowledge, and of producing poetry, with that renewed enthusiasm burning fiercely within him . . . At Donnington, we are faced with a man who had set goals for himself, and who had every intention of achieving them. And achieve them he did.

Unfortunately, his wife, Elin, couldn't share this enthusiasm, as she had very little Welsh, and it was a great sorrow to him that his four children were brought up in English in spite of his efforts to teach them Welsh.

It was to Lewis Morris that Goronwy turned for guidance and advice, though William and Richard also commented on his

121

work. There followed, between 1752 and 1754, his best writing period. However, the longing for Anglesey wouldn't go away, and he yearned to return there, or, indeed, to anywhere in Wales. The Morris family tried their best to help him, but to no effect. This was when he wrote his well-known *cywydd* expressing his *hiraeth* for Anglesey. Here is Branwen Jarvis's translation of part of it:

> I am far from the land of my fathers,
> Woe is the telling of it, and from my own dear Môn;
> In the place where I used to play,
> There are men who do not know me;
> A friend or two remember me,
> A mere couple, where once there was a hundred;
> I am a man isolated, and of no account,
> And to the land of Môn I am a stranger;
> A stranger to our old expressive tongue,
> A stranger to the sweet song of the muse . . .
> Great is my lamenting for her,
> Like unto Zion is Môn to me.

In 1755 Goronwy and his family moved to Walton near Liverpool. In April of that year his daughter, Elin, died at the age of 17 months. His moving elegy to her is one of the best known of his works. Perhaps it was sympathy with his grief that made Richard Morris encourage him to move to London to become secretary to the Society of Cymmrodorion, where he was able to mix with his more cultured compatriots. Members of this convivial gathering met every month in London taverns, but their underlying purpose was more serious than mere carousing. Lewis Morris stated that its main aim was 'the Cultivation of the British Language and a Search into Antiquities'. According to Branwen Jarvis, the fundamental point about the Cymmrodorion and Goronwy's whole-hearted delight at his inclusion in its activities is that it is a public and corporate mirror image of Goronwy's own spirit. She says:

> On reading Goronwy's letters, one is constantly aware that he is a man with a serious and wide-ranging mission. He wishes to know all there is to know of Welsh language and literature and

antiquities. He wants that knowledge to be perceived in the light of scholarly principles . . . The founding of the Society, and Goronwy's poetry and criticism, are two important facets of what has been rightly described as the eighteenth-century renaissance in Wales.

Soon after arriving in London he wrote a self-mocking poem, sometimes referred to as 'The Garret Poem'. In it he describes the town noises around him, of pedlars shouting out their wares, the raging quarrels of prostitutes in the street beneath him, while he may cultivate his muse in the quiet of his garret, even though he owns little else but a full mind.

It was here that he wrote his best-known poem, a *cywydd* in praise of Anglesey, which, in spite of its loving description of the leafy meadows of his native county, is more of a hymn of praise to God and a tranquil acceptance of God's will for him:

> When Môn and her gentle beauty
> Shines red-hot from the heat of the flame,
> And her bulging silver veins
> And her lead and iron are aflame,
> To what avails shelter from the molten earth?
> May God provide a home for the soul!
> A fine shining house of glory
> In the fortress of the Stars, in the Holy choir;
> And there chanting aloud
> Their brilliant song to the beloved Lord
> May the Men of Môn be, and Goronwy,
> Henceforth unable to take their leave.
>
> (Trans. Branwen Jarvis)

But as soon as he arrived in London he was in trouble. Lewis Morris complained of his 'positiveness', adding, 'and positiveness will not always do, though we are in the right'. William now writes to Richard of his concern not only for Goronwy's drinking but also for that of his wife, Elin: 'A bishopric is little enough where the wife be constantly thirsty.'

It was about this time that Lewis and Goronwy seriously quarrelled, a quarrel which lasted until Lewis's death, when Goronwy wrote an elegy to him, full of sorrow and praise of his mentor. The reason for the quarrel is not certain but it may have

123

been because Lewis refused to give him any more money. Goronwy's answer had been to attack his erstwhile friend and benefactor in a vicious poem called 'Cywydd i Ddiawl' (*Cywydd* to a Devil).

It was time for Goronwy to take flight again, this time to Virginia, where he was offered a position as Master of the Grammar School at the College of William and Mary in Williamsburg. The salary of £200 a year was tempting, and once again, his penchant for getting himself into trouble had sealed his fate.

He and his wife and three sons sailed in December 1756, only Richard, the most loyal of the Morris brothers, seeing him off. It must have been an horrific voyage, with thieves and prostitutes for companions. All they had to drink was dirty water. Elin and the youngest child, Owen, fell ill and died, and were buried at sea. It was virtually the end of Goronwy as a poet. The elegy to Lewis Morris was his only composition in America. In the words of Branwen Jarvis, Goronwy the writer, did not, in any significant way, survive the journey to America.

The twelve years he spent in Virginia, before his death in 1769, were as stormy as anything he had known back home. It wasn't long before he and another master at the college were charged before the College Board with drunkeness and unseemly language. His companion was sacked, but Goronwy got in first by resigning. He found himself a living in Brunswick County, probably through new connections arising from his marriage to a Mrs Clayton, Matron of William and Mary, who was a sister of the President of the Foundation. Goronwy's second marriage didn't last long for his wife died within a year.

Wife number three was Joan Simmons. By this time Goronwy's circumstances had changed for the better. In addition to his living he now owned a four-hundred acre tobacco plantation complete with four negro slaves. But drink was still his master, for in 1765 the local records show that he was yet again charged with drunkeness and unseemly behaviour. An American encyclopaedia refers to him thus at this time:

His curacy there was worth £35 per annum to which were soon added a house in the churchyard and £6 for the superintendence of the school. He was now in fairly good circumstances, but his health was not good, and he visited Liverpool [Virginia] taverns more frequently than was desirable.

He was profoundly a child of his own times. His poetry and the literary opinions expressed in his letters are a reflection of the classicism of the age which emphasised learning and art above romanticism. Goronwy was scathing about the folk-verse which was being collected at the time by people like Lewis Morris. The Welsh writer he seems to have admired most was Ellis Wynne. When he moved to Walton the only book he had taken with him was *Gweledigaethau y Bardd Cwsc*. This is not surprising. He of all people could appreciate its satirical thrust.

In Welsh literary history Goronwy, traditionally, finds his place among the poets. Yet Branwen Jarvis finds him rather more than a poet. He was an important writer of prose. His poems, she considers, are restricted, restrained, disciplined by the calls of tradition but,

. . . with his letters, we are altogether in a freer, less hidebound world. He writes with a racy, colloquial vigour, direct and earthy, occasionally bawdy. Their pace, variety and liveliness were nevertheless prepared with care and deliberation in the eighteenth-century manner.

IOLO MORGANWG (1747-1826)

Here it seems right to mention their younger contemporary, that unique figure, Iolo Morganwg (Edward Williams). To describe him as a prolific writer is to understate his vast output throughout his long life—as a poet in both English and Welsh and as a tireless promoter of ancient Welsh history. Born in Llancarfan in the Vale of Glamorgan in 1747, he spent most of his life in nearby Flemingston where his father was a stonemason, which was how Iolo himself also earned his living. His mother, Anne Mathew, related to one of the local manor-house families, was a cultured but penniless woman who imbued him with a passion for books and learning. He began to collect and copy old manuscripts, mainly with the aim of proving the importance of Glamorgan in the annals of Welsh literature. His enthusiasm at times led him to let his all too vivid imagination run riot, probably assisted by a partiality for laudanum.

As Dr Prys Morgan points out in his book on Iolo in the Writers of Wales series, he was one of the earliest Welsh scholars to see the value of folk culture, such as the maypole and Morris-dance culture of eighteenth-century Wales, particularly of his native Vale of Glamorgan, and he bitterly denounced the Methodists for destroying it.

In 1781 he married a farmer's daughter, Margaret Roberts, a lively, literate, intelligent woman, who, says Dr Morgan, understood him to perfection. But he went through her inheritance in no time and the couple had to

Iolo Morganwg

126

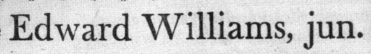

Edward Williams, jun.

MARBLE-MASON,

A T

Flimſton, near Cowbridge ;

MAKES all Sorts of *Chimney-pieces, Monuments, Tombs, Head-ſtones,* and every other Article in the MARBLE and FREESTONE-MASONRY, in the neweſt and neat-eſt Manner, and on the moſt reaſonable Terms.

As he has for many Years regularly followed this Trade in *LONDON* and other capital Towns under the beſt Maſters, he hopes he will be found capable of executing any of the above Articles to the Satisfaction of all who may be pleaſed to honor him with their Commands, and on cheaper Terms than thoſe who profeſs the Trade without ever having followed it where any tolerable Knowledge of it could be acquired.

As there are various Sorts of good *Marble* found in many Parts of GLAMORGAN, *Monuments, Tables, Chimney-pieces,&c.* of it may be had very cheap,

Marble Tables, Chimney-pieces, &c. clean'd and new poliſh'd on reaſonable Terms ; alſo Letters cut on old *Monuments,* or *Tombs.*

Orders directed to him at *Flimſton,* or at the *Printing-Office,* or to Mr. *Bradley,* at the *Horſe and Jockey,* in *Cowbridge,* will be duly attended to.

R. THOMAS, PRINTER, COWBRIDGE, 1779.

Iolo Morganwg (Edward Williams) advertising his craft and wares

flee from one place to another, Iolo eventually landing in the debtors' prison in Cardiff for over a year. Here he began to set his reams of writings in order. He had already spent some years studying and imitating the poems of Dafydd ap Gwilym, and

127

he now sent specimens to members of the Gwyneddigion Society in London, claiming he had discovered them in obscure local manuscripts. These, and his accounts of Druidic history were seized upon with delight and Iolo was acclaimed a great scholar. When he came to London in 1791, says Dr Morgan, he posed as a Welsh 'character' in London drawing-rooms, an authentic 'Welch bard', self-taught, poverty-stricken, a child of nature. He organised a Druidic *Gorsedd* on Primrose Hill in 1792, composing prayers and bardic degrees for the occasion. Much later, in 1819, his delight knew no bounds when, for the first time, the *gorsedd* became officially part of the National Eisteddfod held that year in Carmarthen.

Almost a hundred years were to elapse before later scholars began to cast doubts on the authenticity of his claims for the druidic antiquity of Welsh history and, more seriously perhaps, on the Dafydd ap Gwilym poems he had 'discovered'.

It was Professor Griffith John Williams who first doubted the authenticity of much of Iolo's work. Dr Morgan described how, when the papers were given to the National Library in 1916, the young scholar began to work on them, his approach being always two-pronged:

He spent his lifetime pointing out clearly the terrible forgeries of Iolo, and just as much time showing the Welsh people that Iolo was perhaps their most extraordinary visionary. He began to rehabilitate Iolo as a romantic lyric poet as early as 1919. He admitted Iolo's great importance as a radical . . . in 1926, the same year as he published his revelations on the forgeries. He continued this double approach, though one suspects that gradually he had come to have an admiration, even a veneration for Iolo's genius. To those who knew G. J. Williams there was something touching in the way he had developed something like humility before Iolo's character.

THE HYMNWRITERS

In the year 1735 something happened in Wales which was to have a deep and lasting effect on the character and history of the country. That was the year in which two young men, quite independently of each other, became passionately convinced of their mission to attack the spiritual poverty, as they saw it, of the Anglican Church to which they both belonged. One was Howell Harris, a schoolmaster at Talgarth in Breconshire, the other was Daniel Rowland, a clergyman at Llangeitho in Cardiganshire.

It was a time of religious revivals in many countries, both in Europe and America. Soon John Wesley was to start out on his preaching journeys, but by this time Harris and Rowland had got together and had already set much of Wales afire with their own revivalist mission. They began to organise 'Societies' (*Seiadau*) where members could listen to their preaching which was concerned above all with a theology of redemption and personal relationship with Christ. A vast number of people experienced a great change in their spiritual lives, and, in the words of R. T. Jenkins, a country where the Anglican Church had been weak soon became a country of Welsh chapels. At the same time it must be remembered that, although they attacked the Church, these early Methodists still remained within it. It was the Church itself which rejected and eventually expelled them.

In 1737 a twenty year old medical student happened to hear Howell Harris preach in Talgarth churchyard. That scene has entered into the myths of Welsh Methodism, and indeed of Welsh literature, for William Williams (William Pantycelyn as he is best known) was so overcome by what he heard that day that he decided to leave medicine and enter the Church. He was ordained deacon in 1740, but that was as far as he got, for his association with the Methodists was known and frowned upon. He now decided to join Daniel Rowland as an itinerant preacher, for by this time a serious rift was developing between Harris and Rowland, Harris eventually withdrawing to the community he had founded at Trefecca.

William Williams (1717-91)

However it is as a writer that Williams Pantycelyn is best-known in Wales, not only for his expressive hymns which still move us today, but also for his two epic poems, written in the plain language of his native Carmarthenshire and influenced by his reading of English Puritans like Milton and Bunyan.

A collection of his hymns was published for the first time in 1744 under the title *Aleluia*. These were mostly in Welsh, but some were in English, and other collections followed, some 800 hymns in all. Professor T.H. Parry-Williams once said in a radio talk:

Those of us who rather thoughtlessly enjoyed singing these popular hymns in our youth, probably had little idea of the daring mystical nature of some of his ideas, nor did we fully comprehend the spiritual vision of the Methodist movement which they expressed—the constant portrayal of a pilgrim wandering from an Egyptian world to a Canaan above, beyond the dark far-distant hills; the holy lust (*trachwant* as R. Williams Parry put in his sonnet) for a Beloved as expressed in the Song of Solomon.

And Saunders Lewis went as far as to call him the first of the great writers of the Romantic Movement in European literature.

Of his two epic poems perhaps the better known is *Bywyd a Marwolaeth Theomemphus* (The Life and Death of Theomemphus), published in 1764. It is, according to the author himself, a story of a sensitive and sensuous youth, one with a lively imagination and powerful passions. Williams had no sympathy at all with those who knew nothing of such passions. In it the poet is taken up to a high mountain to have a complete view of the course of Theomemphus's life. (Does that remind you of Ellis Wynne's Sleeping Bard?)

Theomemphus is born in the Land of Nod and is shown

130

breaking every possible known divine commandment. He it was who had been in Sodom and Gomorrah. He was one of Herod's soldiers, killing the children. He was the Prodigal Son, who had carved the Cross, who had been one of those calling out 'Crucify Him!' Then follows a sudden terrifying vision of God's judgement when an angel descends from heaven to denounce him. Theomemphus listens to the angel and to the various theological voices of the day with deepening despair, until at last he is comforted by Evangelius who preaches forgiveness and love.

He then falls in love with the beautiful and good Philomela, but the angel is there to cast doubts on the purity of his love, for it is Satan who has sent her. In great torment he gives her up. In his comprehensive book in the Writers of Wales series Dr Glyn Tegai Hughes suggests that this is a justification for priestly celibacy, adding that this seems rather strange coming from a married priest whose eighth child has just been born. But Williams explains this as a warning to the young to mistrust the passions. (I can't help wondering what Philomela felt about all this.)

Dr Hughes says:

> The language of the poem is often rough, but there's an unflagging drive which carries the story along and an intensity that casts memorable lines from often unpromising material . . . It is the epic of evangelical Calvinism with its hard-eyed view of human nature, its alternations of despair and rejoicing, its God and self-centred coherence . . . What the poem still does is persuade us that, behind the arid detail, principles of the utmost vigour reside. The language is frequently careless and all too often falls into bathos, yet there are passages of emotional force with moments of breath-taking grandeur.

He was also a considerable writer of prose. When Saunders Lewis said that Williams Pantycelyn was closer to young present-day novelists than was the nineteenth-century novelist Daniel Owen, he may have been thinking of *Ductor Nuptiarum* . . . written in the form of a dialogue between Martha and Mary. Martha has made a disastrous marriage, led by the flesh rather than the spirit. Her husband has turned out badly and, because of the way she looks now, he has lost all interest in her. Mary's marriage, on the other hand, is described in glowing terms, for it is based on a love developed by the love of God. What is particularly interesting is the idea of equal partnership and responsibility between male and female in an age when masculine supremacy was taken for granted.

Then again there is *Llythyr Martha Philopur* (The Letter from Martha Philopur), which deals with the problems of Christian conversion. The letter opens on a note of joy at Martha's discovery of Christ's forgiveness of her sins. 'It is as difficult for me to be silent now as it is for a woman to be silent when giving birth.' Full of joyful enthusiasm, she seeks approval from her teacher, Philo Evangelius, who writes back to her counselling caution, as nothing, he warns, is as simple as it seems. There is no work of God without Satan trying to lay a finger on it. She is warned that outward signs of joy and emotion can be misleading. There are sometimes doubts whether such feelings can come from God. Martha's letter gave expression to certain moral and psychological problems encountered by the young revivalists not only of that time, but of all time.

The Society, or *Seiat*, was an important factor in early Methodism, as, indeed, it continued to be until fairly recently, and it was Williams who gave it shape and order. Saunders Lewis said that, after two centuries of apathy and confusion, when Wales was once more being stirred by religious experience, it was found necessary for mental health to resurrect some form of confessional of the Catholic Church, and this, he said, is what the *Seiat* was.

The aim of Williams Pantycelyn was not so much to be considered a good and elegant writer, but rather to foster the spiritual growth thrown up by the Methodist Revival. Some have said that he wrote in far too much of a hurry to be concerned with art. Dr Derec Llwyd Morgan would contest this, maintaining that Williams' style showed that he understood the importance of variation, comparisons and new poetic measures. Above all, what becomes clear is his deep understanding of human nature and all the heat of its passions. Dr Morgan sums up the importance of Williams Pantycelyn thus:

132

He devoted his indisputable gifts as a writer to give shape to the Methodist movement, to assist its members to understand it and to teach them to use this new power as a basis for their whole living.

'Rwy'n edrych dros y bryniau pell
    Amdanat bob yr awr;
Tyrd, fy Anwylyd, mae'n hwyrhau,
    A'm haul bron mynd i lawr.

Tyn fy serchiadau'n gryno iawn
    Oddi wrth wrthrychau gau,
At yr un gwrthrych ag sydd fyth
    Yn ffyddlon yn parhau.

'Does gyflwr dan yr awyr las
    'Rwyf ynddo'n chwennych byw;
Ond fy hyfrydwch fyth gaiff fod
    O fewn cynteddau 'Nuw.

I look across the distant hills,
    Hour upon hour I wait;
The sun is almost set, my dear—
    Come, for it groweth late.

Pull my heart's fondness, all compact,
    From fickle things away
Unto the One whose faith is sure
    For ever and for aye!

Under the blue sky nothing is
    That love of life affords,
But satisfaction stays within
    The house that is my Lord's.

(Trans. Anthony Conran)

ANN GRIFFITHS (1776-1805)

The other great Welsh hymn-writer, born in the eighteenth century, was a woman—Ann Griffiths, born Ann Thomas, in 1776. She died in 1805 following the birth of a child, who died a fortnight after the mother.

Like Williams Pantycelyn, Ann was born into a comfortable farming family at Dolwar Fach, which is in the hill country between Dolanog and Llanfihangel yng Ngwynfa, not far from Llanfyllin in Powys. She and her family were members of the Estab-lished Church, but her father and two brothers fell under the influence of Methodism. Ann, however, was a more reluctant convert. She had tended to mock those she saw going off to a meeting at Bala. 'Look at those pilgrims on their way to Mecca,' she is reported to have said.

It was also said that she was fond of dancing and singing to the harp. One day, on her way to a dance at Llanfyllin, she happened to meet an old servant of her mother's, who persuaded her to go to a preaching meeting instead. The sermon she heard there affected her profoundly. But Ann wasn't one to rush into things and it was a whole year before she finally became converted to Methodism. She had tried to remain within the Church, but a story is recounted of her having gone to the *Plygain* (a kind of midnight Mass) when the vicar invited her round for breakfast. It appeared that his conversation on that occasion was not altogether delicate, which was enough to drive Ann away from the Church, eventually to join the Methodists. This incident happened in 1796 when she was twenty years old.

Another member of the *Seiat* was a man called John Hughes, known everywhere as John Hughes, Pontrobert. A very close friendship developed between him and Ann. Some said he was in love with her, though Saunders Lewis disputes this ('unfashionably', as he said). There was certainly much letter-writing between the two, but this was confined to spiritual matters. Saunders Lewis suggested that the rigid social difference at the time between them would have ruled out any idea of a closer association. John Hughes was her theological mentor. Theology was the only bond between the two. Eventually John married Ruth, Ann's maid, and she herself married a wealthy farmer, Thomas Griffiths.

The extraordinary thing was that Ann, for some reason or other wrote down only a few verses of the hymns she had composed. Instead she would recite them to Ruth, who, remembering them by heart, in turn sang them to John Hughes. He was the one who wrote them down so that we have them today.

The books to read in English about Ann Griffiths are two by Canon A. M. Allchin, one in the Writers of Wales series, the other, *The Furnace and the Fountain*, published 1987 by the University of Wales Press. Canon Allchin said that when he first heard of her hymns, he had been so impressed he decided to learn Welsh in order to understand them better. Her works are, of course, rooted in the Bible and the Book of Common Prayer. Figures and metaphors from both illuminate every line, as for example in the hymn, '*Rhyfedd, rhyfedd, gan angylion*', which Saunders Lewis said could be regarded as 'one of the majestic songs in the religious poetry of Europe'. This is Canon Allchin's translation of two of the verses:

> Wonderful, wonderful in the sight of angels, a great wonder in the eyes of faith, to see the giver of being, the generous sustainer and ruler of everything that is, in the manger in swaddling clothes and with nowhere to lay his head, and yet the bright host of glory worshipping him now.

When Sinai is altogether on smoke, and the sound of the trumpet at its loudest, in Christ the Word I can go to feast across the boundary without being slain; in him all fullness dwells, enough to fill the gulf of man's perdition; in the breach, between the parties, he made reconciliation through his self-offering.

Here are some of my own impressions in reading her hymns. First of all I am always struck by the pictures she paints. Undoubtedly Saunders Lewis was right to talk about her intellectual gifts but, instead of describing intellectual concepts difficult to understand, Ann gives us visual metaphors, almost film-like. Notice all the pictures in this one:

> Bererin llesg gan rym y stormydd,
> Cwyd dy olwg, gwêl yn awr
> Yr Oen yn gweini'r swydd Gyfryngol
> Mewn gwisgoedd llaesion hyd y llawr;
> Gwregys euraidd o ffyddlondeb;
> Wrth ei odre clychau'n llawn
> O sŵn maddeuant i bechadur
> Ar gyfri yr Anfeidrol Iawn.

> Cofia ddilyn y medelwyr
> Ymhlith 'r ysgubau treulia d'oes.
> Pan fo mynydd Seina'n danllyd
> Gwlych dy damaid wrth y Groes;
> Gwêl ddirgelwch mawr duwioldeb,
> Cafwyd allor wrth dy droed,
> Duw a dyndod arno yn diodde,
> Llef am ole i ganu ei glod.

> Pilgrim weary of the tempest
> Lift thine eyes and see above
> The Lamb become a mediator
> In lovely ground-length garments clad,
> A golden belt of faithfulness
> Adorned with bells a-ringing with
> A song of pardon for the sinner
> Achieved through his Immortal Love.

> So go and follow after reapers,
> Among the sheaves now spend thy day;

When Mount Sinai is a-blazing
Soak thy morsel at the Cross;
See the mystery of the Godhead,
There's an altar at thy feet,
On it God and man doth suffer,
Cry for light to sing his praise.

And it is not only visual figures she employs. The other senses
are there also:

Mae sŵn y clychau'n chwarae
    Wrth odre Iesu mawr
Ac arogl pomgranadau
    I'w clywed ar y llawr.

The sound of bells are playing
Around the feet of Jesus,
And the scent of pomegranates
Arises now from the earth.

Secondly, there are the paradoxes she employs:

Rhoi Awdur bywyd i farwolaeth
A chladdu'r Atgyfodiad mawr.

The Author of life is put to death and the Great Resurrection
is buried.

Dŵr i nofio heb fynd trwyddo.

Water to swim without reaching the other side.

Fy enaid trist wrth gofio'r frwydr
Yn llamu o lawenydd sydd.

My sad heart, recalling the battle, leaps with joy.

But, above all, Ann Griffiths is concerned with the Person of
Christ, and the contemplation of His love. There is no indication
that her conversion made her more socially aware, no mention
of giving to the poor or tending the weak. What she did do in
her poetry was describe the wonder of Christ in a way which
can only be called mystical.

137

How did other people see her? We have one portrait of her which can be accepted as reasonably accurate, showing a high forehead and deep, expressive eyes. According to John Hughes she was taller than average and had great dignity. There have been many attempts to portray her both in books and plays, not all avoiding the danger of vulgarising her life by introducing a fictitious love story. One novel, however, much praised by Saunders Lewis, is *Fy Hen Lyfr Cownt* by Rhiannon Davies Jones, which has all the hallmarks of authenticity and was awarded the Prose Medal at the National Eisteddfod some years ago.

All we have left of Ann are some 72 verses, one letter in her own handwriting, and seven letters carefully copied out by John Hughes. One wonders why he went to the trouble of copying them out when they were actually addressed to him. Had she wanted them returned?

Tecwyn Lloyd in an interesting article refers to the man who became her husband, Thomas Griffiths. A nebulous character, he says, whose features are impossible to discern (although John Hughes did write a biography of him in 1840). After the marriage, the correspondence between Ann Griffiths and John Hughes, in which they had discussed so many theological matters, ceased, and there is no evidence that she wrote anything at all after that. Saunders Lewis and Canon Allchin both felt that she would have become a nun had she lived centuries earlier. Did she feel that her marriage had come between her and her burning need for Christ?

As with most of the writers I've mentioned in this book I've been struck by the difference of opinions along the years of various critics about her works. Professor W. J. Gruffudd called her an 'intuitive mystic' in that least mystical of all forms of religion, Methodism. Saunders Lewis emphasises her intellect. She was a perceptive woman with a fine brain, he says, well able to cope with theology. He maintained that it was theology and not mysticism which inspired her. She had a mind like Plato, adding, rather more contentiously from my point of view, that she wrote like a man. Thomas Parry-Williams, on the other hand, tends to throw cold water over all the praise. Her poems, he says, are a patchwork of quotations from the Bible, most skilfully woven together. She was, he said, a tailor of words.

Be that as it may, one is left filled with wonder at the achievements of this young girl from Dolwar Fach.

THE NINETEENTH CENTURY

In looking through Welsh writing of this period you could be right in thinking that here was a very solemn, sober century. On the other hand it certainly was what Thomas Parry called the most copiously productive time in the whole history of Welsh literature. An enormous number of periodicals were started, a host of religious books were printed, memoirs of great men (and some not so great) found their way to people's homes, for by now, of course, there was a growing number of readers. But today's critics realise that something stultifying happened to creative writing at this time, no doubt partly occasioned by all those theological disputations and strict Victorian ideas of morality.

Throughout the country so much was happening, there were so many educational, social and political changes, all of which should have stimulated the Welsh artist. But he appeared to have lost focus, unable to find an original voice throughout the upheavals of the century. Poetry, especially poetry in the strict metres was, in the main, turgid and seemed to have lost any connection with real life. Much of it was derivative, imitating its more successful English counterparts.

What had happened? In his book on the period, 1850-1914, *Codi'r Hen Wlad Yn Ei Hôl*, Hywel Teifi Edwards suggests that this crisis of confidence developed from a reaction to the traumatic 'Blue Books' Government Report on Education in Wales in 1847. So—a word of explanation, to begin with, about what became known as *Brad y Llyfrau Gleision* (The Betrayal of the Blue Books). The three young English commissioners responsible for the report, while praising the work of the Welsh Sunday Schools, deplored the ignorance of Welsh school children (who, being for the most part monoglot, could barely understand their questions in any case). The commissioners' solution was—a completely English-based education.

That was irritating enough to lovers of the language, but what incensed Welsh Nonconformists in particular was the attack made on Welsh morality, the commissioners having apparently accepted uncritically the prejudices of certain Welsh Anglican clerics, angry at the growth of Nonconformity throughout Wales, and the impression was given that the Welsh were unique in their dishonesty and sexual immorality. Although this part of the report occupied little more than a few lines, it was immediately pounced upon by London newspapers, feeding already built-in prejudices, and putting Nonconformist Wales on an angry defensive, bordering on hysteria. Hywel Teifi Edwards states that, from that time on, Philistinism, with its undervaluing of intellect and imagination, and its emphasis on commercial values, had a field day in Wales. Getting on in the world became all-important, and there was a frenetic eagerness to prove that, of all the nations of the vast Empire, Wales was the godliest, most virtuous and most loyal. (A comprehensive chapter on the Blue Blooks appears in *Mid-Victorian Wales* by Ieuan Gwynedd Jones.)

Inevitably it was poetry that suffered most from this attitude. In the increased moral atmosphere, the poet was regarded as an unacceptable *outré* element at a time when Wales was striving to regain universal respect. The Eisteddfod, in particular, had to show that Welsh loyalty was no threat to the unity of Britain, and could therefore be happily supported by the wealthy, anglicised aristocrats in Wales, with the result that hardly anything that was unacceptable to the nonconformist conscience got published in the second half of the century.

Whereas in the old days the leaders of Welsh cultural life had been the princes, followed by the nobility, those leaders were now ministers and preachers, who tended to disapprove of the old culture the common country folk knew and loved—the interludes, the ballads, the *penillion*. These were now replaced by hymns, and the emphasis was on Bible reading, almost to the exclusion of everything else. Abstract points of doctrine acquired all-pervading importance. There were theological arguments between different sects, and the bitterness between the Established Church and Nonconformists, mainly political by now, became explosive. For the many who loved literature, worst of all was the general ignorance of the nation's literary past. Some of the Methodists, in particular, regarded anything written before their Revival as being intrinsically evil, and a definite hostility towards learning developed in some Methodist circles, although this was hardly true of the leaders, such as Thomas Charles and Thomas Jones.

Does this sound unfair? It is the opinion of Thomas Parry in his book, but I think many now share his views. And certainly trying to wade through the century's *awdlau* is pretty hard going, although some, such as the young Eben Fardd's 'Dinistr Jerusalem' (1824) have distinct merits. Saunders Lewis praises the work of the Llanystumdwy poet, Robert ap Gwilym Ddu (Robert Williams). Other writers, such as R.J. Derfel, argued the need for a Welsh university, National Museum and Library. Samuel Roberts's *Farmer Careful of Cilhaul* (1850) saw the beginning of attacks on landlordism, when the newspaper, *Baner Cymru*, took up the cudgels. Such was the poverty in rural Wales at that time, it resulted in emigration to America and Patagonia, fired by the writings of people like Samuel Roberts.

During this time ballads continued to be produced and printed in booklets of 4-8 pages, and these were often sung at fairs. They were hardly great literature, but they did reflect important aspects of the age, such as social distress, landlord oppression, love and courtship (though by now the coarser ballads of the eighteenth century had become unacceptable), shipwrecks, transportation, the evils of strong drink and, most popular of all, murders.

In an article on ballads in *Cof Cenedl*, VI (from which I've had all the following information) Tegwyn Jones tells us that the ballad singers were often women. There was Mari Ellis, who, in 1822, sang of the Irish troubles, and Rebecca Williams, who sang of Madocks building the Cob at Porthmadog, and about 'the horrible murder of Mary Jones' by Thomas Edwards, the *Hwntw Mawr,* who had come from south Wales to work on the Cob. Then there was another, by one Mary Roberts, in praise of the bravery of the Marquess of Anglesey at Waterloo. Another singer, called Maria Williams, always ended her ballad by singing this verse:

Os gofyn neb yn unlle
Pwy wnaeth y geiriau hyn?
Hen wraig fach anllythrennog
Heb fedru darllen dim.
Ni fedraf ddim sgrifennu
Na darllen hefyd chwaith
Neu buasai'r gân yn brydferth
Yn dod i ben ei thaith.

Should anyone ask who composed these words—an illiterate little old woman who cannot read at all. I can neither read nor write, otherwise this would have become a really fine song before it reached its journey's end.

The king of the ballad singers was undoubtedly a blind harpist called Richard Williams (Dic Dywyll), an Anglesey man. This is how he was described by Charles Herbert James in his book *What I remember about myself and old Merthyr*:

He would stand in the middle of the street on a Saturday night, ballads in hand, a penny a piece, and begin to talk, setting everybody in a roar with generally some allusion either to some

Richard Williams and Hugh Pugh (on horseback) returning home after visiting the Cardiff Eisteddfod, 1834

143

comical person in the neighbourhood, or some queer circumstance that was tickling the imagination of the people. When he found he had got an audience, and all were in good humour, he would begin his singing. He is credited, and I have no doubt truly, with having stopped the building of a workhouse in Merthyr for many years by the effect of his ballad singing, and the feeling he aroused against that form of poor relief.

Tegwyn Jones calls this particular ballad a powerful voice raised against the cruel practice whereby a man and his wife could be separated in their old age. The singer's method was to attack with humour:

Fe gafodd rhai gryn gwrs o sbri wrth wrando Sam Wil Simon
Oedd wrth briodi'n gwneud disgwrs, cyn talu o'i bwrs i'r Person;
'Hyd angau,' dwedai'r ffeiriad ffri, 'cysylltaf chwi â'ch gilydd.'
'Nage, myn diawl,' atebai Sam, 'ond hyd y Workhouse newydd.'

Many at Sam Wil Simon's wedding had a good laugh when they heard what he said to the Parson before handing over the money. 'Till death do I unite you,' said the jolly Parson. 'No, by the devil,' replied Sam, 'only till the new workhouse.'

According to Professor Gwyn A. Williams, Dic Dywyll was one of the speakers who addressed the rioters in Merthyr Tydfil at the time of the hanging of the Chartist Dic Penderyn. He spoke eloquently, calculating the number of people who could be maintained on 15 shillings a week from a nobleman's income of £70,000 a year. Dic Dywyll died in Liverpool, and it is said that his funeral was arranged by a number of Irish people who had cared for him in his last illness.

But to return to the mainstream of Welsh literature. The Eisteddfod grew in importance throughout the century. Prizes were awarded for poems on earnest, theological themes such as The Destruction of Jerusalem, Job, A Consideration of Man's Life, Truth, Contentment, Belshazzar's Feast. Early in the century, as Hywel Teifi Edwards shows in his book, *Yr Eisteddfod 1176-1976* (1976), it was mainly the 'literature loving clergymen' of the Anglican Church in Wales who, by forming a number of regional *eisteddfodau* on the lines of the Cymmrodorion and Gwyneddigion, with their emphasis on history and culture, rescued the Eisteddfod and returned it to Iolo's dream. Maybe the aim of many of them was primarily to offset the influence of Methodism, but their dedication to their native culture was beyond doubt.

There was, of course, an outpouring of hymns, some very good and still sung today. There were also a number of lyrical poets such as Alun (John Blackwell) and Ceiriog (John Ceiriog Hughes) whose works were very popular. Ceiriog had the gift of being able to write words for well-known folk-tunes such as were published in the popular collection *Songs of Wales* (Brynley Richards), but I should add that these poets are not rated very highly today by modern critics.

An exception was the Monmouthshire poet, Islwyn (William Thomas). The death of his fiancée, Anne Bowen, had a profound effect on his whole life. Even though, years later, he married another woman, he could never shake off the loss of Anne, and he nearly succumbed to depression. His friends said that only writing poetry saved his sanity. His long poem, 'Y Storm' (of which he wrote two versions), sought an answer to the tragedies of human experience. This was his way of trying to cope with his own grief. His poems showed the conflict between the mystical on the one side and the orthodoxy of the religion he preached; between adhering to the old theological ideas and opening up to the new.

The years 1840-80 saw the publication of a great number of memoirs, mostly about preachers, all very dignified and very worthy. There was much prejudice against novels, considered a perversion of the truth, even though this was a golden age for the English novel. Those Welsh writers who did venture into those waters often had to justify themselves by introducing a moral theme, such as love of money, the misery of debt or the dangers of strong drink. Dr Thomas Rees, in his *History of Nonconformity in Wales*, wrote in 1861: 'Novels, the disgrace of English literature, and the curse of multitudes of English readers, do not take with Welsh readers.' So it's not surprising that there was a relative dearth of stories and novels at this time. That the picture was not completely black the next chapter will show.

However, there was one man, Owen Wynne Jones, an Anglican priest, writing under the name of Glasynys, who got away from these constraints by collecting a large number of country tales he had heard about bogies and ghosts and fairies. He wrote them down in a vivid prose, using the dialect and colloquial phrases of his native Caernarfonshire.

One other writer whose work has been increasingly recognised as important is Emrys ap Iwan (Robert Ambrose Jones). Born in

Emrys ap Iwan (1851-1906)

Abergele in 1851, the son of a gardener at Bodelwyddan, he spent a short time in Liverpool as draper's assistant before returning to Wales and entering Bala Theological College to prepare for the ministry. His family background was thoroughly Welsh, except that he claimed to have a French great-grandmother, something which obviously influenced him quite a lot.

In 1874, at the age of twenty-three, he went to Lutry near Lausanne to teach English in a private school, a time which he enjoyed enormously, although the work was very hard. Perhaps he could be called the first modern Welsh European. He wrote with enthusiasm of his travels to Rouen, Paris, Fontainbleu, Dijon and Portalier, where, he recounts, he caused some perplexity in the hotel when, confused by the pretty waitress, he asked for *deux boeufs* instead of *deux oeufs*. He later went to Germany to teach English in Bonn and Giessen. His familiarity with French literature (his main models were Pascal and P. L. Courier) had made him intensely aware of prose as a skill, a craft, an art, a conception which was almost absent in Wales at the time.

D. Myrddin Lloyd, in the Writers of Wales series, described the lyrical quality and warmth of feeling of his writing, reminiscent of that of Gruffydd Robert of Milan. The prime enemy, against which he fought throughout his life, was Welsh servility. English was revered as the dominant language. Welsh writing, he said, was riddled with anglicisms and style was turgid and imprecise. His essays on grammar and style are still among the most useful a writer can read today.

On returning to Wales in 1876 he began preaching and writing, mainly for the Welsh Liberal newspaper, *Y Faner*. His sermons, articles and letters to the press were widely read, though not always appreciated, satire being his chosen weapon. He often struck out at Dic Siôn Dafydd, the Welsh equivalent of the Irish Shauneen, a despiser of his own language who loved to parade his scanty command of English and went about trying to ape his masters.

Here was a very important writer whose time for appreciation has belatedly come in the second half of the twentieth century.

DANIEL OWEN (1836-95)

Daniel Owen

Daniel Owen was not the first Welsh novelist. Many a would-be writer throughout the nineteenth century had tried emulating Dickens, Thackeray and George Eliot, but with little success. As we have seen, the trouble was that Welsh Nonconformity tended to look disapprovingly on any work of fiction, calling it fabrication and lies. That was why those who tried to imitate English writers were always conscious of this in the background and felt they had to introduce some moral or other, with often dire results.

In the introduction to one of his novels, Daniel Owen shows the irony of a sincere and God-fearing Nonconformist deacon reading Bunyan's *Pilgrim's Progress* with tears in his eyes while at the same time dismissing a Welsh novelist as one who tells lies to please fools. You could say, however, that he himself suffered from this very constraint in his best-known novel, *Rhys Lewis*, though he did not actually pretend that his was a real autobiography, in spite of calling it that, and writing it in the first person. Towards the end of the first chapter he says: 'Rhys, what shall you say of yourself? Remember to tell the truth.' But somehow we can hear him go on to ask what the whole truth about a man can be, and how is it to be told? Hywel Teifi Edwards said that Daniel Owen was the one Welsh artist of his day to confront this prejudice against the so-called lies of the imagination, and to succeed thereby in convincing his society of a need for a truth about itself which was 'fabricated'.

But what of the man himself? He was born at Mold in 1836. He had little early education, for his family was poor, and the boy's health was poor, too. While he was still a child, his father was drowned in a coalpit accident. Two brothers also lost their lives in the pit, leaving his mother to bring up the four remaining children, supporting them by going out to work. He always considered his mother a remarkable woman and based one of his famous characters on her—Mari Lewis, the mother of his hero, Rhys. The real mother came from the family of Twm o'r Nant, the interlude writer and actor, and Daniel obviously inherited that writer's flair for dialogue and satirical wit.

When he was twelve he was apprenticed to a tailor in Mold, and there couldn't have been a better opportunity for observing people in all their foibles, good and bad. In those days tailors passed their time as they worked in reading to each other, and that is how Daniel got to know the works of Scott, Thackeray and George Eliot. When he was twenty-eight he went to Bala Theological College where he spent much of his time studying English. But after two and a half years he returned to Mold to look after his mother and sister. There could have been another reason, of course. It has been suggested that he became unsure of his vocation, and this could have led to emotional stress. He returned to his old job of tailoring, eventually opening up his own shop. This he combined with a bit of preaching on Sundays, in spite of his confessed horror of public performance.

His first published work had been a translation of an American novelette, *Ten Nights in a Bar Room*. That was when he was eighteen. It was when his health broke down at the age of forty that he was persuaded to write novels. These took the form of serials in a Welsh monthly publication. At once his gift for characterisation and his ear for dialogue became apparent, and his gentle satirical approach showed a promise of things to come.

First came *Straeon y Pentan* (Tales of the Village), a series of short stories. Then came *Rhys Lewis*, built on impressions formed during his own childhood. Although this book gives, at times, an unfavourable picture of religion—'the arrogant self-righteousness that comes from a belief in the personal salvation of the spiritual herrenvolk,' as Professor T. J. Morgan put it—the book also conveys an impression that an era of indubitable greatness (in the spiritual sense) was quickly passing into oblivion. It is still our best introduction to the Wales, particularly that part bordering on England, of the second half of the nineteenth century. There's a vivid account of education in those days, in which he describes a school kept by a savage old soldier with a wooden leg, Robin y Sowldiwr, whose methods were 'treat 'em rough and beat 'em often'. The book is also full of colourful characters living in Mold at that time. It has no main hero. Rather it is a kind of biography of a society.

A basic theme in this and the next two books, *Enoc Huws* and *Gwen Tomos*, is of the child who doesn't know for certain who his father is. But it is extraordinarily difficult to convey any idea of the plot of any of his works, mainly because he was not good at plotting, and most of the novels fall away dismally at the end. For one thing they are far too long, and you get the impression that he had become tired, and was at a loss to know how to bring them to a close.

His second novel, *Enoc Huws*, moves away from the chapel. He is now freed from the constriction he had found there, and his characters are nearly all, if not exactly on the fringe of society, certainly not so bound up in chapel mores. *Enoc Huws* is a portrait of the common man, a grocer, who has made his own way in the world, and is rather a comic character. Life is now a comedy for Daniel Owen, and he has developed a certain sophistication in middle age. Unfortunately once again, towards the end of the novel, it seems as though he suddenly remembers he has to reveal religious truths, and he ends by compromising with the narrow parochialism of the day.

In his last novel, *Gwen Tomos*, he went back to the beginning of the century, and some have said that the portrait of Gwen was inspired by the story of Ann Griffiths. By the time he wrote this he was rather ill. He had always been something of a hypochondriac, and suffered from depression, and now he had money troubles as well. He said in a letter to his publishers that he had great difficulty in knowing how to end the novel but, I find this true of all his novels.

His great theme was men and women as they really are, not as they appear to others. His people sometimes verged on caricature. He himself admitted he wasn't good at construction and his plots often contain coincidences hard to swallow. But one can overlook this as his strength lay in his perceptiveness in outlining his characters and in depicting the society in which he lived.

It is interesting that Wales's first real novelist appeared in a small town near the English border where the people had within them Welsh, English and Irish elements. In the stories we meet preachers and deacons like Rhys Lewis and Abel Huws; radicals like Rhys's brother, Bob, whose beliefs are a source of sorrow to their Methodist mother, Mari Lewis; simple people like Thomas and Barbara Bartley; tradesmen and businessmen like Hugh Bryan and Mr Denman; adventurers like Captain Trefor and Jeremiah Jenkins; people on the fringe of society like Nansi'r Nant; and humorous characters, witty and attractive, like Rhys's 'philosopher' friend, Wil Bryan. Daniel Owen saw the mixture of good and evil in them all.

He saw that most people aimed at becoming members of the rich, middle class. Rather than a society in which everyone was born to his own place, the Victorian age gave the ordinary man for the first time a chance to climb and profit by his own energy and skill and, it must be added, deviousness. The most obvious indication that a man had achieved a particular social status was in his wife and daughters, in their dress, in their ladylike indolence or, as Daniel Owen contemptuously put it, in their 'appearance':

'You well know,' (said Susan Trefor on the day following her 'conversion') 'that I have never baked nor washed clothes, never cooked or ironed, never lit a fire nor done the washing up. I was never taught to do anything but coddle with music, make slipper tops, antimacassars and such rubbish, all the while being given to understand that one day someone important would come along and make a lady of me . . . I am a libel on the name of woman.'

Yet again, some have suggested that the reason he didn't write an unflawed novel was not so much because of the religious narrowness of the period, but because of an innate difficulty in his own character. An essentially gentle man, critical of hypocrisy and greed, tyrrany and vanity, perhaps Daniel Owen himself lacked the fierce passion of a Hardy, a quality surely needed for the writing of great literature. However, his books still have charm for the late twentieth-century reader, and they've made some very good television serials.

EXTRACTS FROM *RHYS LEWIS*

The Corner Shop where I was apprenticed was one of the oldest establishments in town, and Abel Huws, my master, was considered a meticulous fair-minded and far-seeing man. His shop contained general drapery, but his chief trade was in cloth and flannel, which were always of the best quality. In those quiet days there was seldom any bustle in the shop except on fair days, and it is my belief that it was no cause for regret in Abel Hughes's mind that fairs did not occur oftener than four times a year. Yet the Corner Shop was the scene of good and steady trade. It was patronised by old customers whose families had 'dealt' there longer than could be recollected. They were mostly country people, and the majority were Methodists, for those words of Scripture, 'Let us do good unto all men, especially unto them who are of the household of faith', were well observed in those days.

As I remarked, Abel Huws stocked the best quality material, and expected reasonable profit. He never over-praised his wares, and would not reduce the price by a halfpenny. If the customer did not like the goods, he begged him, by all means, not to buy them. I never once heard him 'swear' that this or that material was worth more than he asked for it. Petty lying in business was not so general in those days that any man should find it necessary to 'swear'. I don't believe that Abel Huws ever spent a halfpenny on advertising. The only service that he ever sought from the printer was the making of bill-heads. His shop window was small, and the panes about a foot square, for plate glass had not then come into fashion. What little window-dressing there was could easily be done in an hour, and needed repeating only about a fortnight.

The shop was rather dark even on a bright day, and the smell of moleskin, cotton cord and velveteen was so thick that I felt it could be cut with scissors. When a customer entered, the first thing Abel would do would be to hand him a chair and start a conversation. And that is how the customer would be engaged for half an hour—sometimes an hour, or even longer. But usually he would buy a valuable parcel, and the transaction would end with an invitation into the 'house' to have a 'cup of tea' or 'a bit of dinner'. Very little trade was carried out after sunset, and although the shop was fitted with gas, only one jet was lit—something to show that the shop was not closed. There was very little book-keeping. One book was sufficient, a long narrow one, which served as day-book and ledger, and when a customer paid his account, there was need only to draw a cross in the book in his presence, which served as a receipt.

There was nothing in the business methods of the shop which one could not imagine Noah having performed in the same way had he kept shop before the Flood. And yet Abel Huws was doing well and making money. What would have happened to him today? Yes, today—when people are scheming so much to add to their customers anyhow, no matter how; when winning a customer, and making money are, to many, matters of greater significance than a yard of grey calico.

Will Bryan on the 'Fellowship'

Their surprise was no less when I informed them that Bob's case and mine and Bryan's was to be 'brought before' the Fellowship that night. Beck, being 'Church' had only a hazy notion what was meant by 'the Fellowship' until Will Bryan offered him the following explanation. Will had a remarkable gift for giving the gist of what he was superbly confident that he understood, and this is how he explained to Beck the nature and purpose of our Fellowship.

'It's like this,' said he, 'the Fellowship is a lot of good people thinking that they are bad, and meeting together every Tuesday evening to find fault with themselves.'

'I don't follow,' said Beck.

'Well,' said Will, 'look at it like this: you know old Mrs Peters, and you know Rhys's mother—and it is not because Rhys is present that I mention her—but everybody knows that they are two good-living and godly women. Well, they go to the Fellowship. Abel Huws goes to them, and asks them what they have to say. They say they are very wicked, and guilty of ever so many shortcomings, and Mrs Peters is often in tears as she says so. Then Abel tells them they are not so evil as they think, and gives them counsel, and repeats lots of verses of

153

Scripture, and then he goes to someone else, who in his turn says the same sort of thing, and they keep it up until half past eight when we all go home.'

'There's nothing like that in Church,' said Beck. 'We never hold a Fellowship, and I never heard anyone there running himself down.'

'That's the difference between "Church and Chapel",' said Will. 'You Church people think yourselves good when you are bad, and the Chapel people think themselves bad when they are good.'

Trans. Myrddin Lloyd

TOWARDS TODAY

It takes a long time for writers to assume their proper place in the annals of any literature. Those who are considered unimportant in their own age often achieve a new status in subsequent ages, when the prejudices and hostilities surrounding them have settled. The closer you are to the time of a writer the more difficult it is to assess who is important, whose work is going to be meaningful for future generations.

We have seen that there were all sorts of influences militating against the health of Welsh writing during the last century. Thomas Parry says that the old classical tradition had been interrupted by the social changes throughout the eighteenth and nineteenth centuries as well as newer influences from outside, such as anglicised education, which led to an uncertain grasp of scholarship and of native idioms. There was a lack of proper educational facilities, and a wide class gulf had opened between an anglicised upper class and the Welsh-speaking mass of people. Traces of this situation can still be found even today.

But towards the end of the century things had begun to improve. First of all there was the newly-formed University of Wales, which laid foundations for sound scholarship so lacking during much of the Victorian age. Then came the National Library in 1907, which, apart from its obvious function, became a repository for a large collection of Welsh manuscripts. The most important of Welsh scholars at this crucial time were the philologist, Sir John Rhŷs (1840-1915), and Sir John Morris-Jones (1864-1929) who became Professor of Welsh at Bangor. Not only was he himself a good poet, but he was able to widen the borders of Welsh literature by translating poems from French, German, Italian, Irish, Breton, and even Persian.

Another scholar was Owen Morgan Edwards (1858-1920), who wrote articles and books in a clear style aimed at the ordinary people of Wales. Born to a humble farming family in Llanuwchllyn, his brilliant educational career took him to Oxford, where he was elected Fellow of Lincoln College.

155

Among other works, he edited the popular periodical, *Cymru,* and also a magazine for children, *Cymru'r Plant.* Altogether he had a tremendous influence on the reading habits of the Welsh *gwerin* (the common man).

T. GWYNN JONES (1871-1949)

Fortunately, by this time, Wales seemed to be shaking off the reign of the moralizing preacher. The poet whose work above all took us into the twentieth century was T. Gwynn Jones. At the Bangor National Eisteddfod in 1902 this young journalist was awarded the chair for his *awdl,* 'Ymadawiad Arthur' (The Passing of Arthur). Until this time all the successful poems at the Eisteddfod had been on strongly religious themes, such as Self-Sacrifice and The Creation. These were often long-winded meditations, with little respect for either form or language.

With 'Ymadawiad Arthur', Gwynn Jones took Welsh writing along a different road, albeit a very old one. He went back to the Mabinogion. This probably could not have happened without the impetus given to traditional scholarship by the work of Sir John Morris-Jones. Gwynn Jones was not himself a product of the university, but he had fallen under the spell of this neo-renaissance movement.

Born in 1871 at a farm near Betws-yn-Rhos, near Abergele, his formal education had ended at fourteen. He probably lived at home, helping on the farm when he wasn't reading, writing and studying, until eventually the lure of journalism drew him away from the farm, and he

T. Gwynn Jones

became a sub-editor on the Denbigh newspaper, *Y Faner*, writing occasionally also for *The Liverpool Mercury* and *The Manchester Guardian*. He then moved around various newspapers until in 1909 he became a cataloguer at the recently opened National Library at Aberystwyth. In 1913 he became a lecturer in Welsh at the University College there, and later, Professor.

For a self-taught man, his achievements were tremendous. During his early years at Aberystwyth he translated into Welsh some of Ibsen's plays, Goethe's *Faust* and various Greek and Latin epigrams. He wrote plays, novels and essays; an excellent biography of Emrys ap Iwan, who had been his first employer at *Y Faner*, and also a translation into English of *Gweledigaethau y Bardd Cwsc*.

But it was his poetry that gained him a lasting place in Welsh literature. The chief theme of nearly all his poems is man's search for Paradise, and the need for honour and wisdom in a philistine world. His first published work (in 1902) was *Gwlad y Gân* (Land of Song), in which he poked gentle fun at the Eisteddfod, at the newspaper journalese of the day and at those Welsh who had got on in the world, remembering they were Welsh only on St David's Day.

However, it was the Arthur poem that captured the imagination of young people in particular. It tells of the message of the mortally wounded King Arthur to his friend, Bedwyr (Bedivere). Bedwyr had wanted to accompany Arthur on the barge bearing him to Afallon (Avalon), but the maidens tending the king on the barge say no, he must stay behind, for Arthur is never going to die. Then, as the barge slides away, Bedwyr hears the voices of the three maidens singing of the beauty of the enchanted isle of Afallon. As the music dies away, a fine mist spreads over the lake, shrouding the barge. Then Bedwyr, sorrowfully and silently, returns to the battlefield (see page 159).

What made the poem right for the moment in Wales at that time was that Gwynn Jones had given expression to the hopes of young people in the newly formed *Cymru Fydd* (The Wales To Be), a political and cultural movement aimed at the regeneration of Wales. The poem had broken completely with the pretentious philosophising on truth, progress and eternity of the previous century. Apart from the appeal of the subject, it showed a mastery of both metre and language. It was a tale told in a strong, clear style, and left its imprint on its generation. This is how Thomas Parry assesses him:

> It is to the exquisite facility of his verse and his deep poetic sensibility that Gwynn Jones owes his place among the greatest fine of Welsh poetry, and owes too his amazing gift as a translator . . . Many of his poems are of a meditative, even philosophic cast, but his ideas are in general simple and fairly obvious. He had a passionate hatred of injustice, oppression and avoidable suffering, and an equally passionate love of Wales and her traditions. It was the first that made him, with all his sturdy individualism, into a socialist, and it accounts also for the rather ferocious pacifism—'a pacifist with an emphasis on the fist' was his own description of himself. The state of the world about him, with its wars and miseries, the great slump, and the disappearance of the Welsh speech and Welsh ways from so many parts of the country, gave a biting edge to some of his poems.

One poem, which is really a short play, is 'Tir na n-Óg' (The Land of the Ever Young), an Irish legend, which he wrote in full *cynghanedd*. He had dealt with the theme briefly in an earlier poem, 'Gwlad y Bryniau'—the young man who turned his back on the paradise he had found with his loved one because he could not forget the call of his own land and people. 'Tir Na n-Óg' is the story of Osian, a young poet, who has been out hunting with his companions, and on his way home he meets Nia Ben Aur (Nia of the Golden Hair), daughter of the king of Tir na n-Óg. They fall in love and she takes him with her back to her island home off the coast of Ireland. They live in perfect bliss until Osian begins to remember his home, his hounds and companions, and his longing to return proves too strong. Despite the warnings from Nia that time will catch up with him, he returns, only to find his home in ruins. In trying to help builders replace some of the stones, he falls from his horse. On being picked up he is found to have become a very old man, and instantly dies. It is reminiscent of another Irish legend, The Four White Swans of Lake Derryvaragh. The theme, of course, is man's search for happiness, but when he thinks he has found it, another unhappiness takes its place. The poet, Osian, found his homeland in a sorry state. According to W. Beynon Davies, in his contribution to the Writers of Wales series,

> This can be interpreted as the literary tradition which needs rebuilding, but which can only be done with material from the ruins of the old: in other words, the literary revival must be rooted in the true traditional modes of the language and literary forms.

AFALLON

Draw dros y don mae bro dirion nad ery
Cwyn yn ei thir, ac yno ni thery
Na haint na henaint fyth mo'r rhai hynny
A ddêl i'w phur, rydd awel, a phery
Pob calon yn hon yn heiny a llon—
Ynys Afallon ei hun sy felly.

Yn y fro ddedwydd mae hen freuddwydion
A fu'n esmwytho ofn oesau meithion;
Byw yno byth mae pob hen obeithion,
Yno mae cynnydd uchel amcanion;
Ni ddaw fyth, i ddeifio hon, golli ffydd,
Na thro cywilydd, na thorri calon.

Yno mae tân pob awen a gano,
Grym, hyder, awch pob gŵr a ymdrecho;
Ynni a ddwg i'r neb fynn ddiwygio,
Sylfaen yw byth i'r sawl fynn obeithio;
Ni heneiddiwn tra'n noddo—mae gwiw foes
Ac anadl einioes y genedl yno.

AVALON

Over the wave lies a land of delight
Where grief lingers not, nor time's grey blight;
Men know no pain on that peerless shore,
Caressed by the breezes that play evermore;
Every heart is gay, and life is a song
In Avalon's isle all the day long.

A blissful land with dreams of old
That calmed our fears through ages untold;
Hopes and desires are treasured there,
And the fruits of our travail grow rich and rare;
There shame does not sear, and faith is strong,
And no hearts made weak by an ancient wrong.

On that island's shore burns the pure flame
Of the muse that oft to our poets came
With words of fire that men might arise
From the dust to a nobler enterprise.
Unwearied by age, or by grief and care,
The breath of the nation's life is there.

(Trans. D. Myrddin Lloyd)

R. WILLIAMS PARRY (1884-1956)

This was a poet much influenced by T. Gwynn Jones. Like the older man, he, too, came into prominence when he won the chair at the Colwyn Bay National Eisteddfod in 1910, for his *awdl* 'Yr Haf' (Summer). The poem seemed to embody all that was best in the new poetry, a poem of summer love in a world where, as Bedwyr Lewis Jones described it, the phantom characters come and go in a vaguely medieval setting.

R. Williams Parry

The poet enters an autumnal forest. There he sees, as if in a dream, a sad, elderly man lamenting the death of his loved one. He comes upon a woman, pale and broken-hearted, moaning that her lover has abandoned her now that she is old. A Grey Friar and a White Friar appear in turn, telling the poet that all is vanity and that he should consider his soul and set his sights on heaven. But the poet's reply is defiant:

> Better the love of a maid today than a far-off Canaan tomorrow . . . Sufficient to the day the beauty thereof . . . I desire no better paradise.

In this way the poem is loosely strung together. It is a tapestry luxuriously woven in rich Pre-Raphaelite colours. The grey-haired man in the opening section remembers his beloved as she once was:

> A llyma lun y fun fau;
> Yr oedd fel rhudd afalau,
> Aeron pêr ei hwyneb hi;
> Pa brydwerth o werth wrthi?

161

Cerdded cwr ydfaes, cwrddyd cariadferch,
Ac is lloer ifanc syllu ar hoywferch;
Dod i gyfarfod f'eurferch, fy mun gun
A destlus ei llun hyd ystlyd llannerch.

And this is the likeness of my own fair one:/ like crimson were the sweet berries of her face;/ besides her what beauty had any worth?/ I would walk along the border of a cornfield, I would meet my sweetheart,/ and under a young moon I would gaze on my nimble girl;/ I would come to meet my golden one, my dear maid,/ so dainty alongside the glade.

Saunders Lewis described the poem as 'a series of enchanting love songs, loosely knit together by some pretence of argument full of young Keatsean romanticism'. Well, I suppose such writing can get a bit much, for R. Williams Parry himself later parodied 'Yr Haf' in a poem called 'Yr Hwyaden' (The Duck), in which he made fun of the flamboyant richness of the *awdl* by describing a love affair between Lady Duck and Sir Fox—an affair with a sad ending!

But that was a lot later. 'Yr Haf' became very popular. The three parts of the poem deal with three phases of this symbolic summer. The first, the passing of summer when old age and death overtake love; second, the summer of love where all is joy, and the friars' warning to look to the future is dismissed; third, the evergreen summer preserved in memory and in the hope of another spring. The order is strange. Death comes first. The poem could therefore be interpreted as being about the death of love. Like Hardy, Williams Parry was writing at a time when he was filled with doubts about the notion of a transcendent Providence. He could not accept the reasons offered for the pain of grief and the problem of death.

Seven years after writing 'Yr Haf' he became even more popular with his *englynion* on the death of the poet Hedd Wyn (Ellis Humphrey Evans), the farmer from Trawsfynydd, killed in the battle of Pilken Ridge in August 1917. Shortly before his death Hedd Wyn had posted his *awdl* on 'Yr Arwr' (The Hero) to the National Eisteddfod which was being held that year in Birkenhead. When 'Hedd Wyn' was declared the winner, no one stood up to answer the call of the *Gorsedd* trumpeters. The chair was draped in black. It was a dramatic moment which has entered into the mythology of Welsh literature. The poem Williams Parry wrote afterwards expressed the sadness and bewilderment Wales experienced at that time. It contrasted the gentle peace of the mountains of Trawsfynydd with the violence and grief of death in a foreign field.

After many years of teaching in both north and south Wales, the poet eventually achieved a part-time lectureship at Bangor, but somehow he never got any further than that, possibly, as he claimed, for political reasons. An occasion arose later when he undoubtedly should have been given a full-time lectureship, and his failure to get it caused him much bitterness. He believed he had been passed over because he was not an 'establishment' scholar with a string of publications to his name. He wrote a poem on Goronwy Owen in which he described Goronwy's low, insecure position. In it he asks what would have happened had Goronwy been able to return from Virginia to the Wales of the 1930s. It would have been useless, for the Welsh establishment was still grudging about honouring a poet who chose to write in Welsh. He wrote: *'Pwysicach yw'r chwilotwr/ Nag awdur llyfr o gân . . .'* (A researcher is more important than the author of a book of verse). Somehow the word *chwilotwr* sounds more pejorative in Welsh than in English!

He now withdrew entirely from the Welsh literary scene, refusing even now to allow the Gregynog Press to produce a finely printed volume of his verse. This went on until 1936 when something happened which drew him back. That was when Saunders Lewis, D.J. Williams and Lewis Valentine set a symbolic fire to some outhouses of a bombing school on the Llŷn peninsula, and immediately gave themselves up. The three suffered imprisonment, but Plaid Cymru was re-invigorated and a new patriotic mood swept through much of Wales. The incident had an effect on nearly every Welsh writer who came afterwards. For R. Williams Parry it revived the muse, though only for a time. He was not naturally a public man and his career disappointments had made him even more withdrawn. When he was not teaching he liked to spend his time out in the countryside observing nature. It is said he knew every bird by its call. One day he had gone for a walk with two friends. Suddenly, a fox crossed their path, hesitated briefly, then was gone. His best-known sonnet captures this moment as if in a frozen film (see facing page).

His later works were harsher, full of scorn for man's treachery. He was easily hurt and the ugliness of life distressed him. He had found himself unable to accept the God-centred culture in which he was brought up. He discovered that it was only in nature and in the company of one or two friends that a sort of happiness and calm could be found. This anger against his circumstances affected all the poetry he wrote up to about 1945, and, although he lived for eleven more years, he now wrote little and died in 1956.

Y LLWYNOG

Ganllath o gopa'r mynydd, pan oedd clych
Eglwysi'r llethrau'n gwahodd tua'r llan,
Ac anhreuliedig haul Gorffennaf gwych
Yn gwahodd tua'r mynydd—yn y fan,
Ar ddiarwybod droed a distaw duth,
Llwybreiddiodd ei ryfeddod prin o'n blaen;
Ninnau heb ysgog a heb ynom chwyth
Barlyswyd ennyd; megis trindod faen
Y safem, pan ar ganol diofal gam
Syfrdan y safodd yntau, ac uwchlaw
Ei untroed oediog dwy sefydlog fflam
Ei lygaid arnom. Yna heb frys na braw
Llithrodd ei flewyn cringoch dros y grib;
Digwyddodd, darfu, megis seren wib.

THE FOX

The summit yards away, as church bells sent
Along the slopes a summons to the parish,
And the splendid sun of July, unspent,
A summons to the mountain—in a flash,
With unsuspecting foot, and soundless trot
Before us this rare miracle came on.
And we, not stirring, each with breath held taut,
Were paralysed; like a trinity in stone
Were standing, when he, too, stood, in a daze,
Stopped in unfrightened mid-step, and across
His single poised paw the fixed double blaze
Of his eyes upon us. Then with no fear, no fuss,
Across the hillcrest slipped his russet fur;
He flared, he faded, like a shooting star.

(Trans. Joseph P. Clancy)

T. H. PARRY-WILLIAMS (1887-1975)

T. H. Parry-Williams

A younger cousin of R. Williams Parry, another poet who became noticed first of all by winning the bardic chair—actually winning the two main bardic prizes at the same eisteddfod, chair and crown. This feat of 1912 he repeated on two further occasions.

He had had a wider education than had his cousin. Apart from his time at the University of Wales, he had studied at Oxford, Freiburg and Paris, and, for a year, had studied medicine and won an award in surgery. He became Professor of Welsh at Aberystwyth in 1920 and was there until 1952.

His first published books were collections of essays, and it was these, together with his sonnets, and what he called his 'rhymes' (*rhigymau*), that is, verses written in an informal style with colloquialisms, which have endeared him to Welsh readers. R. Gerallt Jones (in the Writers of Wales series) has called him 'perhaps the most intellectually gifted of modern Welsh writers, and also the most linguistically spare'. The central themes of his writing were Eryri (Snowdonia), his native heath at Rhyd-ddu, his own family and their connection with the mountain. This he extended to deep philosophising about the natural world around him, comparing it with the decay of ancient loyalties and the fading of youthful idealism.

His popular poem 'Hon' (a title difficult to translate because of its colloquial implications; Joseph Clancy calls it 'This Spot'), is one of his 'rhymes' which gives a good idea of the man, and certainly found an echo in the inner conflicts of many of his readers (see facing page).

166

When he 'passed the scholarship' to go to the County School at Porthmadog, he had to go into lodgings there, for the fourteen miles between school and home were too far for daily travel. Professor Caerwyn Williams described the traumatic effect this must have had on a sensitive boy:

> Those periodic separations from his parents, his home and his native village, probably had considerable influence on his sensitive mind, and perhaps it is not too much to assume that they deepened his awareness of place and time. It is certain that it was at Porthmadog that he first experienced the agony of loneliness and the pangs of home-sickness, which generalised into the feeling of *hiraeth* and of the consciousness of *lacrimae rerum* which seems to have been the chief fountain of his poetic inspiration.

His work often suggests a rejection of any meaning and purpose to life. His interest in science developed the analytical side of his poetry, but throughout there was wonder at the awesome mystery of life.

He had his roots in a monolingual society with an innate love of learning, which he contrasted with a world of modern science, and all its effects on the human mind. Apart from the influence his poems have had on modern Welsh writers, his essays in particular were studied and imitated by scores of young would-be essayists, at least well into the 1950s, by which time that form was beginning to lose its popularity. While these essays give the impression of a leisurely sort of philosophising, we are aware that he is very much in control of what he writes. The combination of sharp intellect, a sensuous mystical quality and direct simplicity of speech was quite revolutionary in the Wales of this time.

HON

Beth yw'r ots gennyf i am Gymru? Damwain a hap
Yw fy mod yn ei libart yn byw. Nid yw hon ar fap

Yn ddim byd ond cilcyn o ddaear mewn cilfach gefn,
Ac yn dipyn o boendod i'r rhai sy'n credu mewn trefn.

167

A phwy sy'n trigo'n y fangre, dwedwch i mi.
Pwy ond gwehilion o boblach? Peidiwch, da chwi,

Â chlegar am uned a chenedl a gwlad o hyd:
Mae digon o'r rhain, heb Gymru, i'w cael yn y byd.

'R wyf wedi alaru ers talm ar glywed grŵn
Y Cymry bondigrybwyll, yn cadw sŵn.

Mi af am dro, i osgoi eu lleferydd a'u llên,
Yn ôl i'm cynefin gynt, a'm dychymyg yn drên.

A dyma fi yno. Diolch am fod ar goll
Ymhell o gyffro geiriau'r eithafwyr oll.

Dyma'r Wyddfa a'i chriw; dyma lymder a moelni'r tir;
Dyma'r llyn a'r afon a'r clogwyn; ac, ar fy ngwir,

Dacw'r tŷ lle'm ganed. Ond wele, rhwng llawr a ne'
Mae lleisiau a drychiolaethau ar hyd y lle.

'R wy'n dechrau simsanu braidd; ac meddaf i chwi,
Mae rhyw ysictod fel petai'n dod drosof fi;

Ac mi glywaf grafangau Cymru'n dirdynnu fy mron,
Duw a'm gwaredo, ni allaf ddianc rhag hon.

THIS SPOT

Why should I give a hang about Wales? It's by a mere fluke of fate
That I live in its patch. On a map it does not rate

Higher than a scrap of earth in a black corner,
And a bit of a bother to those who believe in order.

And who is it lives in this spot, tell me that.
Who but the dregs of society? Please, cut it out,

This endless clatter of oneness and country and race:
You can get plenty of those, without Wales, any place.

168

I've long since had it with listening to the croon
Of the *Cymry*, indeed, forever moaning their tune.

I'll take a trip, to be rid of their wordplay with tongue and with pen,
Back to where I once lived, aboard my fantasy's train.

And here I am then. Thanks be for the loss,
Far from all the fanatics' talkative fuss.

Here's Snowdon and its crew; here's the land, bleak and bare;
Here's the lake and river and crag, and look, over there,

The house where I was born. But see, between the earth and the heavens,
All through the place there are voices and apparitions.

I begin to totter somewhat, and I confess
There comes over me, so it seems, a sort of faintness;

And I feel the claws of Wales tear at my heart.
God help me, I can't get away from this spot.

(Trans. Joseph P. Clancy)

KATE ROBERTS (1891-1985)

Kate Roberts

This novelist, short-story writer and journalist was born in Rhosgadfan, a small quarrying village near Caernarfon, which has been the source and inspiration of nearly all her work. Here was a completely Welsh-speaking community whose rich language and colloquialisms were reflected in everything she wrote. After graduating at the University College of North Wales, Bangor, she became a teacher in

Glamorgan, first at Ystalyfera, then Aberdare, Cardiff and the Rhondda valley. In 1928 she married Morris T. Williams and seven years later she and her husband bought Gwasg Gee, the publishing house based in Denbigh, and that is where she stayed for the rest of her life, editing *Y Faner*, writing articles, both literary and political, as well as her novels and short stories.

Her talent as a writer was first noticed by Saunders Lewis in 1923 when he wrote to her, praising her increasing mastery of the short-story form in particular. It was probably a word from him that prompted W.J. Gruffydd, editor of the prestigious literary magazine, *Y Llenor*, to ask for, and publish her first story, 'Y Llythyr'. Many more followed, and in 1925 this resulted in her first volume, *O Gors y Bryniau*, followed by *Rhigolau Bywyd* (1929) and *Ffair Gaeaf* (1937). An English translation of some of these stories appeared in 1946 under the title *A Summer Day*.

Her first novel, *Traed Mewn Cyffion* (Feet In Chains), published in 1936, was prompted by her memories of the First World War, when her brother was killed. Writing it was, for her, a necessary act of therapy for her continuous grief at his loss. Although it was generally very well received, it was something of a disappointment to her that Saunders Lewis's initial reaction had been rather lukewarm. He told her, after he had read the first draft of it in 1934, that he felt the grasp of the craft of novel-writing was not as sure as that of her short stories. She defended herself furiously in the otherwise warm correspondence that had grown between them over the years, but whether or not a kind of hurt was the reason, the fact remains that she wrote no book for publication until *Stryd y Glep* in 1949, followed by a spate of novels and short stories, her last, *Haul a Drycin*, appearing in 1981, when she was ninety.

Although her literary work is not overtly political—she concentrated more on the reactions of ordinary quarrying folk to events, and their hard struggle to survive—her journalism was devoted to Welsh nationalism and literary criticism. Her letters to Saunders Lewis from the Rhondda spoke of her religious agnosticism at that time. Neither she nor her husband had wanted to get married, she said. They would have preferred to have lived together without that church wedding they went through at Llanilltud Fawr. But in her writing she always succeeded in portraying the strength of the old Puritan culture of her childhood, and especially the tragedy that can occur in trying to block out emotion. Indeed, in later life she returned to the chapel, and became a popular Sunday School teacher.

Her novels could be said to be divided into two periods, though the two are inextricably connected. The first, her early ones, are imbued with her love for the slate-quarrying community of her childhood, in which she identified with her people's hardships, and admired the Puritan values which enabled them to cope. The novels of the second, her Denbigh period, are rather more complicated and introspective, as Derec Llwyd Morgan points out in his volume in the Writers of Wales series. There is now a deep unhappiness about the materialism and nihilism of today's more prosperous society, as the author sees it in small town life in Wales.

Her home meant a great deal to Kate Roberts, and her books are full of detailed descriptions of a woman's domestic life and surroundings. Her later novels again reflect her own life, her widowhood, and the loss felt by women who have now perhaps become more comfortably off, but who have lost the support of a society which used to surround and succour them.

A lighter side to her work is shown in her books for children, especially in the charming *Te yn y Grug* (Tea in the Heather). Of the writers who had most influenced her three stand out— Chekhov, Maupassant and, above all, Kathleen Mansfield. Kate Roberts is an important writer whose contained, spare style has influenced many modern Welsh novelists.

D. GWENALLT JONES (1899-1968)

We can now approach the poets of the 1930s, and find a new social awareness pervading their work. Among the more important was Gwenallt (D. Gwenallt Jones), a man born in the mining town of Pontardawe in the Swansea valley. He grew up very conscious of the deprivation caused by unemployment in the industrial life of the area, but his family had come originally from rural Carmarthenshire. There was deprivation there, too, albeit of a different kind. Memories of his early back-ground remained with him throughout his life, and indeed they formed the theme of his last, unfinished novel, *Ffwrneisiau*, published in 1982, many years after his death.

Gwenallt

Small wonder then that he joined the Labour Party at the age of sixteen. This, of course, was during the First World War. At that time there was a ferment of left-wing awareness in the Swansea valley, and this included pacifism and conscientious objection. Gwenallt was still at school, doing part-time work as a pupil-teacher while still studying for his Higher Certificate when he was called up. As a conscientious objector (on socialist, not on religious grounds) he was sentenced to imprisonment at Wormwood Scrubs and Dartmoor, remaining there from May 1917 to 1919. He later published a novel, *Plasau'r Brenin* (The King's Palaces) based on his traumatic experiences there.

On his release he entered a different world when he became a student at Aberystwyth, graduating in Welsh and English and eventually becoming a lecturer there. Although he went through a phase of Marxist atheism, it was to Christian Socialism that he ultimately turned, and his poetry shows a profoundly religious conception of life.

A visit to Ireland in the late 1920s turned him into an ardent Welsh Nationalist. He became a Catholic—Anglican not Roman —and Welsh nationalism and religion are the keynotes to his work. He first captured attention as a poet when his *awdl*, 'Y Mynach' (The Monk), won the Chair at the 1926 National

172

Eisteddfod. The following year, another *awdl*, 'Y Sant' (The Saint) attracted controversy and the Chair was withheld. But his most popular work, without a doubt, was in the more lyrical, short poems, published in five volumes from 1939 onwards. As time went on the later poems displayed an increasing disillusionment, verging on bitterness, with what was happening in Wales. In the beautiful poem, 'Rhydcymerau' (see below), he laments the disappearance of the old life in the home of his forefathers where the forest has taken the place of farm and sheep pastures.

Thomas Parry says that his poems 'show a deliberate avoidance of literary language and poetic imagery, the author consciously aiming at a prosaic manner . . . He does not by any means eschew imagery, but they are images drawn from familiar objects of everyday life.'

RHYDCYMERAU

Plannwyd egin coed y trydydd rhyfel
Ar dir Esgeir-ceir a meysydd Tir-bach
Ger Rhydcymerau.

'Rwy'n cofio am fy mam-gu yn Esgeir-ceir
Yn eistedd wrth y tân ac yn pletio ei ffedog;
Croen ei hwyneb mor felynsych â llawysgrif Peniarth,
A'r Gymraeg ar ei gwefusau oedrannus yn Gymraeg Pantycelyn.
Darn o Gymru Biwritanaidd y ganrif ddiwethaf ydoedd hi.
'Roedd fy nhad-cu, er na welais ef erioed,
Yn 'gymeriad'; creadur bach, byw, dygn, herciog,
Ac yn hoff o'i beint;
Crwydryn o'r ddeunawfed ganrif ydoedd ef.
Codasant naw o blant,
Beirdd, blaenoriaid ac athrawon Ysgol Sul,
Arweinwyr yn eu cylchoedd bychain.

Fy Nwncwl Dafydd oedd yn ffermio Tir-bach,
Bardd gwlad a rhigymwr bro,
Ac yr oedd ei gân i'r ceiliog bach yn enwog yn y cylch:
    'Y ceiliog bach yn crafu
    Pen-hyn, pen-draw i'r ardd.'

Ato ef yr awn ar wyliau haf
I fugeilio defaid ac i lunio llinellau cynghanedd,
Englynion a phenillion wyth llinell ar y mesur wyth-saith.
Cododd yntau wyth o blant,
A'r mab hynaf yn weinidog gyda'r Methodistiaid Calfinaidd,
Ac yr oedd yntau yn barddoni,
'Roedd yn ein tylwyth ni nythaid o feirdd.

Ac erbyn hyn nid oes yno ond coed,
A'u gwreiddiau haerllug yn sugno'r hen bridd:
Coed lle y bu cymdogaeth,
Fforest lle bu ffermydd,
Braitiaith Saeson y De lle bu barddoni a diwinydda,
Cyfarth cadnoid lle bu cri plant ac ŵyn.
Ac yn y tywyllwch yn ei chanol hi
Y mae ffau'r Minotawros Seisnig;
Ysgerbydau beirdd, blaenoriaid, gweinidogion ac athrawon Ysgol Sul
Yn gwynnu yn yr haul,
Ac yn cael eu golchi gan y glaw a'u sychu gan y gwynt.

RHYDCYMERAU

The seedlings of the third war's trees have been planted
On the land of Esgeir-ceir and the fields of Tir-bach
Near Rhydcymerau.

I remember my grandmother in Esgeir-ceir
Sitting by the fire and pleating her apron,
Her complexion sere and yellow as a Peniarth manuscript,
And the Welsh on her lips the Welsh of Pantycelyn.
She was a scrap of last century's Puritan Wales.
My grandfather, though I never saw him,
Was a 'character'; a mite of a man, brisk, tough, bouncy,
And fond of his pint;
He was a straggler from the eighteenth century.
They raised nine children,
Bards, deacons, and Sunday School teachers,
Leaders in their small circles.

My Uncle Dafydd farmed Tir-bach,
A *bardd gwlad* and the region's rhymester,

And his song to the bantam was famous round about:
   'The bantam cock goes scratching,
   Now here, now there, in the garden.'
I would go to him on summer holidays
To tend sheep and compose lines of *cynghanedd*,
Englynion and eight-lined stanzas in eight-seven metre.
And he raised eight children,
The eldest son a minister with the Calvinist Methodists,
And he too fashioned poems.
Our family held a nestful of bards.

And by now nothing is there but trees,
Their impudent roots sucking the ancient soil:
Trees where a neighbourhood was,
A forest where once there were farms.
The debased English tongue of the South where once
Men made poems and talked theology,
Foxes' barking where once were the cries of children and lambs.
And in the dark at the heart of it
Is the English Minotaur's den;
And on branches, as if on crosses,
Skeletons of bards, deacons, ministers, Sunday School teachers,
Whitening in the sun,
And washed by the rain and dried by the wind.

(Trans. Joseph P. Clancy)

WALDO WILLIAMS (1904-1971)

Unlike every poet I've mentioned so far, Waldo Williams was brought up in an English home in Haverfordwest, and was seven years old before beginning to learn Welsh. That happened when his schoolmaster father was moved to the Welsh-speaking rural village of Mynachlog-ddu in north Pembrokeshire. His family's influence on him was very strong. They were Baptists, radicals and pacifists, all of which was to have a direct bearing on his poetry.

Although it was English that he studied at Aberystwyth when he went there in 1923, he began to write little comic verses in Welsh for student *soirées*, mainly because of his friendship with the popular humorous writer, Idwal Jones, with whom he shared lodgings. In such a humble way were some of the best poems of twentieth-century Wales germinated. After leaving university he taught for a time at primary schools in both north and south Pembrokeshire. The tragedy of war weighed heavily on his mind, and his strongly-held pacifist beliefs led him to register as a conscientious objector. He appeared before a tribunal at Carmarthen in 1942, and was released from military service unconditionally.

Waldo Williams

He suffered a great tragedy in 1943 when his young wife, Linda, died barely a year after their marriage, and the following year he left Wales to become a teacher in Huntingdon and Wiltshire. This was where he wrote some of his most profound poetry (in Welsh) during the years following the bombing of Hiroshima and Nagasaki. In a personal gesture showing his opposition to the war in Korea he refused to pay income tax, and was imprisoned on two occasions.

His poems expressing his beliefs in the brotherhood of man and his love of Wales found an immediate response, particularly among young people, when a volume of his collected work, *Dail Pren*, was published in 1956. Quotable lines like 'Daw dydd y bydd mawr y rhai bychain, Daw dydd ni bydd mwy y rhai mawr' (The day will come when little ones will be great, The day will come when the mighty are no more) captured the mood of the 1960s and the young Welsh Language Society. It must be said that some of the other verses in the volume fall rather short of the quality of ones like 'Preseli', 'Adnabod' and 'Mewn Dau Gae'. But, as his fellow-poet, Euros Bowen, said, Waldo was gifted with a sense of humour, and it was all part of his personality, which had to find expression in all sorts of different ways.

But however accessible these verses were, there were others, particularly 'Mewn Dau Gae' (see page 178) which are not easy to understand. A well-known critic, Dafydd Glyn Jones, said that Waldo Williams is possibly the only modern Welsh poet who wrote genuinely difficult poetry. Bedwyr Lewis Jones believed this poem to be one of the finest written in Wales during recent years. The poet himself said that its seeds were sown when, as a boy of twelve, he had had a profound experience when he visited his uncle's farm at Llandysilio in Pembrokeshire:

> In the gap between these two fields, about forty years ago, I suddenly and vividly realised, in a very definite personal experience, that people are, above all, brothers to one another.

At its simplest there are the striking descriptions of nature, what he had observed between these two fields, first in summer, and then on a windy night in November. But it soon becomes clear that a description of scenery forms only a minor part. Amid the curlews and the lapwings the poet had suddenly felt a silence, a silence which shook him to the depths of his being. He tries to understand it by asking questions—What is that sea of light that comes rolling through the dark land? Where did it come from? Who was the marksman? Those who know this part of Pembrokeshire will recognise something of that peculiar incandescent quality of light there which has attracted artists like Graham Sutherland. Asking questions is the poet's way of trying to get at the meaning, groping through a cloud of uncertainty, and the answers don't come easily, although he knows that the answers are there.

There's little doubt that the clue to understanding his work lies in the personality and beliefs of Waldo Williams himself. In 1953 he had become a Quaker, and the poem, completed three years later, is full of Quaker wording: *goleuni* (light); *distawrwydd* (silence); *tawelwch* (stillness): all of which have come to calm the '*oesoedd y gwaed ar y gwellt*' (ages of blood on the grass). In that poem Waldo expressed the conscience and sense of personal responsibility of the Quaker.

Just as a man like Canon Allchin learnt Welsh in order to

study the poems of Ann Griffiths, one hears frequently of people learning Welsh with the express purpose of understanding the poems of Waldo. Professor Caerwyn Williams has said that the word 'prophet' should be used in discussing his work. What more can you say than that?

MEWN DAU GAE

O ba le'r ymroliai'r môr goleuni
Oedd a'i waelod ar Weun Parc y Blawd a Parc y Blawd?
Ar ôl i mi holi'n hir yn y tir tywyll,
O b'le deuai, yr un a fu erioed?
Neu pwy, pwy oedd y saethwr, yr eglurwr sydyn?
Bywiol heliwr y maes oedd rholiwr y môr.
Oddi fry uwch y chwibanwyr gloywbib, uwch callwib y cornicyllod
Dygai i mi y llonyddwch mawr.

Rhoddai i mi'r cyffro lle nad oedd
Ond cyffro meddwl yr haul ym mydru'r tes,
Yr eithin aeddfed ar y cloddiau'n clecian,
Y brwyn lu yn breuddwydio'r wybren las.
Pwy sydd yn galw pan fo'r dychymyg yn dihuno?
Cyfod, cerdd, dawnsia, wele'r bydysawd.
Pwy sydd yn ymguddio ynghanol y geiriau?
Yr oedd hyn ar Weun Parc y Blawd a Parc y Blawd.

A phan fyddai'r cymylau mawr ffoadur a phererin
Yn goch gan heulwen hwyrol tymestl Tachwedd
Lawr yn yr ynn a'r masarn a rannai'r meysydd
Yr oedd cân y gwynt a dyfnder fel dyfnder distawrwydd.
Pwy sydd ynghanol y rhwysg a'r rhemp?
Pwy sydd yn sefyll ac yn cynnwys?
Tyst pob tyst, cof pob cof, hoedl pob hoedl,
Tawel ostegwr helbul hunan.

Nes dyfod o'r hollfyd weithiau i'r tawelwch
Ac ar y ddau barc fe gerddai ei bobl,
A thrwyddynt, rhyngddynt, amdanynt ymdaenai
Awen yn codi o'r cudd, yn cydio'r cwbl,

Fel gyda ni'r ychydig pan fyddai'r cyrch picwerchi
Neu'r tynnu to deir draw ar y weun drom.
Mor agos at ei gilydd y deuem—
Yr oedd yr heliwr distaw yn bwrw ei rwyd amdanom.

O, trwy oesoedd y gwaed ar y gwellt a thrwy'r goleuni y galar
Pa chwiban nas clywai ond mynwes? O, pwy oedd?
Twyllwr pob traha, rhedwr pob trywydd,
Hai! y dihangwr o'r byddinoedd
Yn chwiban adnabod, adnabod nes bod adnabod,
Mawr oedd cydnaid calonnau wedi eu rhew rhyn.
Yr oedd rhyw ffynhonnau'n torri tua'r nefoedd
Ac yn syrthio'n ôl a'u dagrau fel dail pren.

Am hyn y myfyria'r dydd dan yr haul a'r cwmwl
A'r nos trwy'r celloedd i'w mawrfrig ymennydd.
Mor llonydd ydynt a hithau a'i hanadl
Dros Weun Parc y Blawd a Parc y Blawd heb ludd,
A'u gafael ar y gwrthrych, y perci llawn pobl.
Diau y daw'r dirháu, a pha awr yw hi
Y daw'r herwr, daw'r heliwr, daw'r hawliwr i'r bwlch,
Daw'r Brenin Alltud a'r brwyn yn hollti.

IN TWO FIELDS

Where was it from, the sea of light that came rolling
Its deep upon Weun Parc y Blawd and Parc y Blawd?
After I had questioned long in the dark land,
Where did he come from, the one who has always been?
Or who, who was the archer, the sudden enlightener?
The field's life-giving hunter was the roller of the sea.
From on high, above the clear-piping curlews, the prudent
    darting of the lapwings,
He brought me the tremendous stillness.

He stirred me to the depths where all that stirred
Was the sun's thought measuring the haze,
The ripe gorse on the hummocks clacking,
The host of rushes dreaming the blue sky.

Who is calling when the imagination wakens?
Rise, walk, dance, behold the universe.
Who is hiding himself in the heart of the words?
All this, on Weun Parc y Blawd and Parc y Blawd.

And when the great fugitive and pilgrim clouds
Were red with the evening sunlight of a November storm
Down in the ash trees and the sycamores that separated the fields
There was the song of the wind and a depth like the depth of silence.
Who is there, amid the pomp and the pageantry?
Who is standing there, comprehending all?
Witness of every witness, memory of every memory, life of every life,
Tranquil soother of a troubled self.

Till at last the whole world came to the stillness,
And on the two fields his people walked,
And through them, among them, about them spread
A spirit rising from hiding, conjoining all,
As it was with the few of us once, in the plying of pitchforks
Or the tedious tugging of thatch out on the heavy moor.
How close to each other we came—
The silent hunter was casting his net about us.

O, through ages of the blood on the grass and through the light the
   lamenting,
What whistling heart alone heard? O, who was it?
Deluder of all arrogance, tracker of all trails,
Heigh! the eluder of armies
Whistling recognition, recognition until there is recognition.
Great was the leaping as one of hearts freed from their hard ice.
There were fountains bursting towards the heavens
And falling back, their tears like the leaves of a tree.

On this the day ponders under the sun and cloud
And the night through the cells of its thickly-twigged brain.
How still they were, the night and its breath
Over Weun Parc y Blawd and Parc y Blawd unhindered,
Holding fast to the object, the fields full of people.
Surely the coming of what must will come, and in that hour
The outlaw come, the hunter come, the claimant come to the gap,
The Exiled King come, and the rushes part.

(Trans. Joseph P. Clancy)

180

SAUNDERS LEWIS (1893-1985)

Saunders Lewis

When Saunders Lewis died in 1985 it was as though an exciting era had come to an end, not just in Welsh literature, but in twentieth-century Welsh history. During his lifetime he produced polar reactions throughout Wales and beyond, both to his actions and writings. People revered him or reviled him, for his stand as a Catholic Nationalist was unswerving, uncompromising, and, indeed, sometimes unexpected.

It is difficult to discuss him as a writer without reference to his politics. He himself told us that it was through Yeats, Synge, Colum and other Irish writers that he first came to understand the meaning of nationhood. Then, when he was a soldier in France during the First World War, he discovered the work of the French writer, Maurice Barrès, and that made him resolve to read Welsh literature extensively and acquire a mastery of the language. Home on leave he picked up a copy of T. Gwynn Jones's biography of Emrys ap Iwan, and this clinched everything. Dafydd Glyn Jones, in his article in *Presenting Saunders Lewis*, says:

> He set out to sell nationalism to a people who were shy of practising it, and a brand of nationalism which he must have known was too sophisticated for most people to understand.

He was born in Wallasey in 1893, the son of a Calvinistic minister. He was privately educated, and then became a student at Liverpool University until the outbreak of war, when he volunteered immediately and obtained a commission. In 1918 he returned to Liverpool and graduated with first-class honours in English. His book, *A School of Welsh Augustans*, was

181

a version of the research he did as a student. In 1922 he became lecturer in Welsh at Swansea and later married an Irishwoman whose family had come from Wicklow to Liverpool. Her family were Wesleyan Methodists, but in 1932 he followed her into the Roman Catholic Church.

In 1936, with two others, he set fire to outhouses at the RAF bombing school which had been recently established in the Llŷn peninsula. The three men immediately reported themselves at the nearest police station and, after their first trial was moved from Caernarfon to London, they were each sentenced to nine months imprisonment. On his release Saunders Lewis was dismissed from his post as lecturer at Swansea, and from 1937 to 1952 he lived mainly on teaching, journalistic work and some farming, until he was made lecturer again, this time at Cardiff.

In 1962 his radio lecture, *Tynged yr Iaith* (The Fate of the Language) resulted in the formation of the Welsh Language Society, devoted to the rescue of the endangered language, by means of civil disobedience. As Saunders Lewis said later, he saw it grow into something even bigger than he himself had envisaged or even hoped for.

From the literary point of view, his works span drama, novels, poetry, journalism and crticisim. As a dramatist he can be considered among the foremost writers of Wales. He himself has said that the only sort of creative writing that appealed to him was drama. All the same, as Geraint Gruffydd says in the introduction to the collected poems (selections have been sensitively translated by Joseph Clancy), at the heart of all his writing is a deep consciousness of language, its music, sound and rhythm, which he captured in a variety of poetic forms. There is in his poetry a richness of imagery, fed not only by all he had experienced in his long and heroic life, but also by his tireless reading of Welsh and European literature.

The wonders of nature are a constant theme, as well as his passion for Wales, which is all part of his love of humanity. Saunders Lewis's Wales is always seen as part of Europe, but this feeling for his country is often tinctured by disappointment and anger, even despair. As Dr Geraint Gruffydd points out, this love was never expressed in an overt, sentimental patriotism, but in a more subtle way, by praising those he revered, those in the present as well as in the past. The two loves, that of nature and Wales, can best be understood by a third factor, his Catholic religion. This again is not displayed in a direct way, but rather through poems to saints or characters from the Bible.

His first play, *The Eve of St John* (1921), is his only play in English. It is a whimsical one-act play, set among the peasantry of nineteenth-century Wales, and is obviously influenced by Synge. It was many years later, in 1937, that his first powerful play, *Buchedd Garmon* (The Life of St Germanus), was written. This was a radio play, based on the supposed visit of the saint to Wales in the year 429, to combat the heresy of Pelagianism, the doctrine that man can by his own efforts achieve perfection. He felt the moral in it for a Wales, racked by disunity and threatened by materialism, was clear. This was followed by *Amlyn ac Amig*, based on a French Christmas legend, and then, in 1947, he completed *Blodeuwedd*, which many feel to be his finest play.

The theme is the clash between love and lust. In creating the beautiful Blodeuwedd from flowers, the magician, Gwydion, had omitted to give her a sense of right and wrong. She could therefore be hardly held responsible for her actions. On the other hand, her lover, Gronw Pebr was able to choose between right and wrong, and he must therefore be punished. As Bruce Griffiths says in his contribution to the Writers of Wales series, Blodeuwedd is a tragic figure who inspires pity and revulsion, comparable to Phedre, Lady Macbeth and the Medea of Euripides. Elsewhere (in *Presenting Saunders Lewis*) Dr Griffiths says:

> Blodeuwedd ironically has a significance today probably undreamt of by the author—it strikingly depicts the catastrophic results of 'scientific' meddling with the natural order of things.

The next play, *Siwan*, is not unlike *Blodeuwedd*, for it is based on the adulterous liaison between Siwan (Joan), daughter of King John, and wife of Prince Llywelyn the Great, and her lover, Gwilym Breos, a powerful Norman marcher lord. The third act, in which Llywelyn and Siwan are reconciled, is almost unbearable in the intensity of emotion it evokes.

With *Gymerwch Chi Sigarét?* (Have a Cigarette?) Saunders Lewis comes to the twentieth century. The play is based on a true story, when a Russian agent, sent to assassinate a man by means of an explosive cigarette case, chose instead to defect to the West, because of the scruples of his Catholic wife. The dilemma of Marc, the hero, is that, if his mission fails, he will lose Iris to the Secret Police. If he succeeds, he will lose her anyway, as she has vowed she will never marry an assassin. The plight in which Marc and Iris find themselves is an example of evil in the world, and the question is, how can all the suffering be reconciled with faith in a loving God?

Brad (Treason) is another play based on a true story. This was the abortive *putsch* to kill Hitler in 1944. The play reveals the varying motives of those in the plot and their reactions to their failures. It is a powerful play whose universal appeal goes far beyond Wales.

Esther is based on the Old Testament story and, as in all Saunders Lewis's plays, finds a parallel dilemma in the world of today. In *Cymru Fydd* (Wales To Be) he returns to modern Wales. This play is about a kind of Jimmy Porter character, showing the cynicism of the disillusioned idealist.

Of his two novels, the first, *Monica*, was published in 1931. It was dedicated to the memory of Williams Pantycelyn (he had, four years previously, published a startling biography of the hymnwriter). The novel was an imaginary development of the character of Martha, the woman governed by lust depicted in Pantycelyn's *Ductor Nuptiarum*. *Monica* was given a very hostile reception in the Wales of the time, for it dealt with hitherto taboo sexual themes, although written with great sensitivity. It was twenty years or so before its worth was recognised and even longer before it was given a second edition.

Merch Gwern Hywel, the other novel, is completely different. It is about Sarah Jones, the author's great-grandmother, who eloped with William Roberts, a young Methodist preacher from Anglesey. Their marriage represented a fusion between two classes of society, i.e. that of the eighteenth-century Anglican landowners and the young lower class Methodist leaders of the early nineteenth century. (This novel has been translated by Joseph Clancy under the title *The Daughter of Gwern Hywel*.)

I am very conscious of how incomplete is my list of writers in the first half of twentieth-century Wales. There are still many, dramatists like Kitchener Davies, poets like Euros Bowen, novelists like Caradoc Prichard, who deserve whole chapters to themselves. But as the title of this book indicates, this is merely a dip into Welsh literature. I hope it has encouraged readers to find out more for themselves.

WELSH LITERATURE TODAY*

These last months of thinking about—and soaking myself into —present-day Welsh literature have made me only too aware of the enormity of the task I had so blithely agreed to a couple of years ago. Anyone in Wales who hasn't been a cultural Rip Van Winkle for the past ten years or so will be aware that something explosive has happened to Welsh writing during this time.

First, though, I'd better warn you that I'm no academic. I've never studied Welsh language or literature at the feet of some distinguished Gamaliel of the University of Wales, or anywhere else for that matter. So you may be wondering what qualifications this person has to venture hold forth on such a subject in a place like this. Well, apart from being a novelist, most of my professional life has been spent in journalism, particularly in radio. I know people think that journalists get away with a lot, but I did have to become adept at sifting through and presenting other people's opinions on the most abstruse topics and try making them comprehensible to others like myself. In the course of which I couldn't help forming one or two opinions of my own. But most of what I'm going to say is based on the careful work of brilliant critics like Dr John Rowlands, Professors M. Wynn Thomas, R.M. Jones and others, whom I'll try to acknowledge as I go along.

As to evaluating present-day writers, I'm sure you'll appreciate that it's rather too early to discuss their work in depth. He/she who is acclaimed today may be derided tomorrow, and most of them haven't yet had time to realise their potential, or indeed their limitations. So when I do name certain people, it is in order to illustrate a point I am making, and not necessarily according to their importance as writers. Just as well to get that clear!

Let me begin by stating the obvious. In Wales we are a two-language nation. Notice that I don't say we are a bilingual nation. That would rather indicate that everyone in Wales

*A lecture delivered to the Celtic Congress in Bangor, 22 July 1996

speaks two languages, which is patently untrue. We live in a country where the vast majority speaks English only, and where the minority language has to fight a perpetual battle against apathy, unconcern, prejudice and sheer ignorance.

Is that going it a bit strong? I don't think so. Not so long ago the then Secretary of State for Wales dismissed Welsh as being 'a private language'. What did he mean? How did he say it? Since I didn't actually hear him, but merely read the report in a newspaper (and that's a dangerous thing to do, I admit) I have no way of knowing whether it was said as a joke or as a serious perception. But the fact remains that this attitude is not confined to Secretaries of State. You do meet it rather a lot, particularly in the more anglicised areas of Wales even today.

This could account for a certain unease that has existed throughout most of this century between those in Wales who write in Welsh and those who write in English. But, paradoxically, it all probably first came into the open during the First World War with the publication of two works of fiction— *My People* and *Capel Sion* by Caradoc Evans, in which, in a highly quixotic style, the writer portrayed the Welsh as a bunch of bizarre, immoral hypocrites, living by their own crazy rules. These highly acclaimed books (that is, highly acclaimed in England) were published in London, but the howls of rage that went up in Wales were compounded by the knowledge that the author was no ignorant Englishman who could perhaps have been ignored, but was a Welsh-speaking writer from the depths of Cardiganshire. How dared he? A tremendous furore ensued, notwithstanding the fact, as Hywel Teifi Edwards has pointed out, that, forty years earlier, that much-revered Welsh-writing novelist, Daniel Owen, had been equally if not more critical of Calvinistic hypocrisy, only that he expressed it less flamboyantly, in a much less quirkily burlesque style.

A lot of water has passed under the bridge since then, and by today there is a new perception of the work of Caradoc Evans and, indeed, of other writers in English like him. All the same, during the 1930s there was a vast gulf between 'them' and 'us', with Saunders Lewis in particular expressing concern about the dangers of English-writing in Wales. His particular *bête-noire* in a famous lecture in 1938, was the term 'Anglo-Welsh'. Most of these writers, he claimed, wrote in an English regional tradition, centred on the industrial life of the south with little reference to the rural north, so that the concept of Wales as one nation was alien to them. Harri Pritchard Jones, though a well-known admirer of S. L.'s work, says it is a pity that he seemed unaware of the way these Valleys writers were developing a new colourful, idiomatic, Welsh Englishness with roots deep in the rural life from which most of them had sprung, though losing their language on the way.

At the same time something else happened in the 1930s. Two new publications came on the market—Gwyn Jones's *The Welsh Review* and *Wales,* edited by that colourful journalist, Keidrych Rhys. (The nationalist poet, Harri Webb, became his assistant at one period.) In these a new, more friendly Welsh orientation was encouraged, giving space to the work of Welsh-speaking writers who wrote in English. (You will notice that I'm trying to avoid the unpopular, but useful term 'Anglo-Welsh'.) It was here, I believe, that the work of Emyr Humphreys and R.S. Thomas first saw the light of day.

By today Caradoc Evans's work is going through a kind of rehabilitation in Wales. Perhaps he could be called our first Welsh post-modernist with critics like Gerwyn Wiliams assessing his influence on one of the best novels to have come out of Wales this century—*Un Nos Olau Leuad* by another Caradoc, Caradog Prichard. By the time this work appeared in 1961 writers in Wales were at last beginning to appreciate the creative value of an escape from realism. No writer writes in limbo. He/she is always influenced by what has gone before, even though this influence may be subconscious. The trouble is, as Gerwyn Wiliams has observed, less skilful writers have tried to imitate Caradog Prichard's use of the vernacular, not always successfully. This is how the novel opens. (There is an English translation, but my point can only be made in Welsh.) A little boy is talking to the Queen of the Black Lake:

Mi a i ofyn i Fam Huw gaiff o ddŵad allan i chwara. Gaiff Huw ddŵad allan i chwara, O Frenhines y Llyn Du? Na chaiff, mae o yn ei wely a dyna lle dylet titha fod, yr hen drychfil bach, yn lle mynd o gwmpas i gadw reiat 'radeg yma o'r nos. Lle buoch chi ddoe'n gneud dryga a gyrru pobol y pentra 'ma o'u coua?

Nid ni sy'n 'u gyrru nhw o'u coua, nhw sy'n mynd o'u coua. Fuo ni'n unlle ddoe dim ond cerddad o gwmpas. Trw bach! Trw bach! ges i'r peth cynta'r bora, yn nôl gwarthag Tal Cafn o Ben y Foel a hel llond cap o fyshirŵms ar Ffridd Wen ar ôl codi mymryn bach o datws Now Gorlan i Mam ar y ffordd adra

There aren't many who can imitate that sort of writing successfully. A cult can end up as a kind of comic stereotype. Novelist Mihangel Morgan has fun imitating the style of these writers 'yn smalio shgwennu fatha plentyn bach mewn tafodiaith a chael getawe!'

One danger is—though I'm now inclined to change that to 'one danger has been'—that in the sensitive political situation this century, some writers may have been put off portraying Wales with a truthful but damaging warts and all presentation. I think it's safe to say that most of our authors have been inspired by political conviction and nationalistic beliefs. But these very beliefs can also inhibit and impede a writer who wants to follow his own artistic integrity. In her early years, Kate Roberts herself had some difficulty with this, not only because she didn't want to harm the nationalistic cause, but because of her own Calvinistic background which checked her writing about religious doubts and sexual frustrations. By the time she had come to write the fine novel of her later years, *Tywyll Heno* (1962), she was ready to express her disillusionment with some of the sacred cows of her youth. Gerwyn Wiliams has suggested that it's possible that up to this time she had been constrained by the memory of the embarrassed outcry which had greeted Saunders Lewis's novel, *Monica*, in the 1920s, dealing with a sexual theme.

Shortly after the war came T. Rowland Hughes whose readable novels whetted the appetite of Welsh readers for more. They paved the way for Islwyn Ffowc Elis, whose novels were —yes, popular—but so much more than popular. He respected the language enough to give it a modern dignity. His books are certainly entertaining, but they have a deeper function. As he himself put it:

A man needs to belong to a patria, be that defined as a neighbourhood or as a small nation-state (which I believe Wales should be), to a community, be it as small as a family or as numerous as a small nation (which Wales is), to a creed-bearing movement, be it religious or political or whatever, and/or to God.

His books gave a tremendous impetus to reading Welsh novels. Not only this, they also gave inspiration and confidence to a number of new novelists who published in the 1960s, '70s and '80s.

But it's time I moved on to the 1990s. So what is the general situation today? The growing importance of the National and Urdd Eisteddfodau has encouraged fledgling writers to try out their wings, and the winners have benefitted, perhaps not so much financially, but certainly from the resulting publicity. One of our most innovative young novelists is William Owen Roberts, whose novel, *Y Pla,* has been translated into several European languages. Still, he does feel bitter about the ignorance of our closest neighbour about Welsh writing. 'Nothing is taught in English schools about Wales, its history and literature,' he says in *Peripheral Visions: Images of Nationhood in Contemporary British Fiction*, edited by Ian A. Bell:

I find even amongst intelligent and enlightened English people a great ignorance. Can any English author imagine getting up in the morning to sit at a desk for eight hours to write in a language which has no official status in its own country? Can any English author imagine writing in a language which might quite easily die and disappear as a daily living tongue in the first few decades of the next century? This is why I have begun to feel recently that writing in Welsh is a classic twentieth-century experience. You are writing on the edge of a catastrophe.

I think all of us who write in Welsh are familiar with these moments of near despair. Why do we do it? Certainly none of us writes for the money. If we're honest, what we want above all is recognition. It doesn't matter in the end whether your work pleases or irritates. What we want is to have people take notice. Possibly that is why some of our youngest poets, who are equally at home in both languages, those like Gwyneth

Lewis, Huw Jones and Einir Jones, have recently published volumes which contain poems in both Welsh and English. This is no problem for Gwyneth Lewis for one. She loves writing in both, and says that almost unconsciously it's the theme which dictates which language the poem should be written in. She's had the experience of starting a poem in one language and almost immediately knowing that this is the wrong one for this particular poem, and so had to switch to the other.

Some other young poets are worried by this trend. Iwan Llwyd has said that the implications are far more tragic for the future of Welsh literature than whether or not there's to be a bar at the National Eisteddfod, a topic which has occupied reams of space in the media throughout the year. He writes in *Barddas*:

> This suggests . . . that Welsh culture no longer offers them a challenge and confidence of a clean page in their own language . . . If our young people cannot respond to this new, clean page in their own language, then there will be no Welsh language in the new millenium.

And another poet, Emyr Hywel, can see a time coming when these poets will no longer have any need of Welsh in which to express themselves. So they stifle their unique identity and turn their backs on the strength and vision their language has given them.

Poet Menna Elfyn is aware of these problems. She recognizes that there is a growing urge to explain ourselves to the outside world, to a world where people no longer need reminding that there are voices other than English within these islands. It's an ironic fact, isn't it, that the prestigious literary festivals in Wales like Hay-on-Wye, and yes, the UK Year of Literature at Swansea last year, gave scant attention to Welsh-language writing. As I write these notes comes the news that the present Conservative Government has inflicted an unkind wound—no, that's not strong enough—a *vicious* wound on us, by torpedoing the EU agreement for awarding £8 million aimed at promoting minority languages in Europe. This would have encouraged the translation of our literature into other languages. It's a funny sort of world where this sort of decision is left to an English

Lord whose knowledge of our language is non-existent. Here I'm tempted to read this little poem by Mike Jenkins, which, I think, says it all:

THIS HOUSE MY GHETTO

Why does 'Cymru'
stick to my tongue?

And the other 'Wales'
undo its meaning
and flow naturally?

I hear the word
abused on television
'Come—rye'
Or 'Come—roo' even

Just after the Japanese Premier
Has been pronounced perfectly.

I'd like to say it without thinking
I'd like to stop explaining
Where we are in Europe.

Like R.S. Thomas, Menna Elfyn believes strongly that a poet can write in only one language. R.S. says that he can write prose in Welsh, but no poetry. Menna Elfyn has addressed the problem by publishing her Welsh poems side by side with their English translations, as in her recently published *Eucalyptus* (1995) and *Cell Angel* (1996).

What it all means is that we can't get away from a growing awareness of how ignorant other people are about us, but it's only now we are beginning to realise that it's up to us to do something about it and push away at our frontiers. I suspect that this new awareness has given rise to a greater under-standing at last between English and Welsh writers here.

Richard Poole, a lecturer in English at Coleg Harlech, is well placed to judge. He has just relinquished the editorship of *Poetry Wales*. In an article in the weekly magazine *Golwg* he welcomes this new phenomenon and maintains that the two languages will be stronger together than apart. They should not be in opposition to each other. It's an unhealthy situation, he says, where two languages seem to be spending time just scoring points over each other. Sadly, this does happen but perhaps we're on the verge of a new beginning.

Since their formation, the two Academies, Welsh and English, have had their ups and downs in mutual understanding. But in recent years, under the wise direction of their respective chairpersons, Sally Roberts Jones and Harri Pritchard Jones, there's been a healthy closing of the gap. Tony Bianchi, the Literature Director of the Arts Council of Wales has also played an important part in reconciling the two sides of the Welsh cultural coin. Recently, the Welsh Academy has relaxed its former rule about limiting the number of members to what had been called an academic elite. The new system has meant an influx of lively, articulate young writers, all ready to tear apart the proverbial sacred cows.

And for those of you who read Welsh, there's no better assessment of the whole situation than in the recently published *Diffinio Dwy Lenyddiaeth Cymru* (1995), edited by M. Wynn Thomas.

But let's think about some of the more specific aspects of writing in Wales. How do people get to know about us? Where are our books discussed? What about the creative process in radio and television? And, of course, theatre.

Let's start at a local level. One of the most important developments over the last 20 years has been the publishing of *papur bro*, the local news sheets which have mushroomed in most parts of Wales, and which are run on an entirely voluntary basis. All right, most of the space is given to the latest doings of Merched y Wawr and memories of old characters and so on. But they've done a tremendous job in keeping those who wouldn't normally read Welsh in touch with their roots, and as far as I can discover, all of them give quite respectable attention to newly published books and their authors.

At the more professional levels there are the weeklies, *Y Cymro* and *Golwg*. (We are still in mourning for the demise of *Y Faner* some years ago, although *Y Faner Newydd* was launched

193

in 1996.) All along the years *Y Cymro* has given honourable attention to books hot from the publishers' presses. A few years ago, a young journalist, Dylan Iorwerth, risked all on a new publication, *Golwg*, aimed at a younger readership, giving space to short stories and poems as well as covering the burgeoning Welsh pop scene. At the beginning we oldies had an ambivalent feeling about the deliberate use of a kind of hybrid, anglicised dialect, presumably to make it all more accessible to the young *gwerin*. But Dylan Iorwerth had his finger on the nation's pulse over that one. He listened, and it's long given way to a more elegant but still very lively style.

The two Bs—*Barn* and *Barddas*—are aimed at a more sophisticated readership. *Barddas*, founded by its editor, the poet, Alan Llwyd, is mainly concerned with poetry, particularly *cynghanedd*, as this has in recent years found a renewed, enthusiastic following among young poets. *Barn* covers a whole range of topics from politics, education, sport to art, theatre and literature. Absolutely vital reading for booklovers—though the title, *Barn*, can be confusing for English farmers. Former editor, Menna Baines, found this out when she kept on getting phone calls— 'Do you sell trailers/fertilizers/feed blocks . . . ?'

For writers, of course, publishers are all important. In addition to the three or four who kept the boat on course all along the years, there are now a number of new, venturesome presses. Professional publishing in Wales made great strides with the advent of the Welsh Books Council which gives publishers vital financial backing and help with publicity. Within their financial resources the Council do a very good job in publicising books. Their bilingual publication, *Llais Llyfrau*, in Welsh on one side and *Books in Wales* in English on the reverse side, is another must for all serious readers. But the Council's resources are limited, and that is why the Government's action in Brussels on 11 June, was such a blow. We all wish more, much more, could be done about translating all our minor Celtic languages into other languages.

But to return to the other periodicals I'd like to talk about. (You see we are quite well served.) There's *Planet*, with it's sub-title *The Welsh Internationalist*; *Poetry Wales* which I've already

194

mentioned, and the lively *New Welsh Review*. The Welsh Academy's quarterly, *Taliesin*, has in recent years lost its rather worthy image, and, particularly under the joint editorship of John Rowlands and Gerwyn Wiliams, it has become much more challenging and experimental, with thought-provoking editorials from each of the editors in turn. For instance, take a look at the current edition (Summer 1996). The editor pulls no punches in castigating (quite rightly, I think) the M.P. for Pontypridd, Dr Kim Howells, for his recent attack on Welsh literary magazines. As John Rowlands says, perhaps it's not a bad sign when a prominent Welsh politician takes this quite vitriolic line. The magazines must be a thorn in the flesh for someone. Dr Howells claimed that the level of subsidy for these magazines (and he particularly mentions *Planet* and *The New Welsh Review*) was ridiculously high compared with their feeble circulation. The grant of £273,050 given by the Arts Council last year is what caused him to send an angry letter to the Secretary of State for Wales about such prodigality. John Rowlands pointed out, with figures to prove it, that the circulation of Welsh literary magazines compares favourably with similar magazines elsewhere in Britain. *Barddas*, for instance, has the second largest circulation in Britain for a magazine devoted to poetry. Welshman Kim Howells should be proud of that. Instead, he complained of 'the moribund and self-obsessed nature of most literary production in Wales', though he himself neither speaks nor reads Welsh.

So you see the enemy is not necessarily over the border alone. It is also within.

Three years ago, the sparky *Tu Chwith* was born, under another joint editorship, this time that of Elin Llwyd Morgan and Simon Brooks, who has subsequently been appointed editor of *Barn*. This magazine with its mainly twenties-something writers is for those who want to pierce through the mysteries of post-modernism. Now, when I first started thinking about this talk I decided that the dread words 'post-modernism', 'deconstruction', 'metafiction' and so on, words which are the source of mystification to most people outside academia, were not going to pass my lips, but I'm afraid these

195

days you can't get away from them, especially if you're going to read *Tu Chwith*.

What is it, this post-modernism? Well, I did get a glimmer of enlightment from Katie Gramich's editorial in *Books in Wales* (Winter 1995). Here's a little of it:

> For some, this monstrous being is like Mary Shelley's creation, a perversion of nature. For others it is an emblem of revolution and liberation. The problem is, the Monster is a shape-sifter who may well look different in Wales from the way it looks elsewhere. If pressed to offer a Rolf Harris version of High Modernism we could sketch in . . . its eschewal of the romantic in favour of the ironic; its experimentation with a destabilisation of language . . . In the Welsh context, some fear that post-modernist texts tend to project a lack of faith in Absolutes or ideas of any kind.

But is this true? I suppose in the end it all depends on what you mean by post-modernism. The post-modernists claim Robin Llywelyn for their own (though I must add that Robin himself once told me that he had no idea what it meant either, and apparently neither does Twm Morys, who is held up as a post-modernist *par excellence*). But both of Robin's novels, *Seren Wen ar Gefndir Gwyn* and *O'r Harbwr Gwag i'r Cefnfor Gwyn* are full of political commitment, though it's not done in a blatant, overt style. You've got to go looking for it. So perhaps he isn't a post-modernist after all. On the other hand, if your definition of post-modernism is an escape from realism, perhaps he is.

Let me give you a taste of Robin Llywelyn's style so that you know what I'm talking about. Here's a selection from his own translation of part of *O'r Harbwr Gwag i'r Cefnfor Gwyn* which was published in *Books in Wales*. Gregor Marini is nearing the end of his search for his sweetheart, Iwerydd, and child, Hunydd. He has reached the Gogledd-Dir (The North Country), which has been laid waste by the invader. The penultimate chapter begins with a description of the ruined houses which are now being rebuilt by the invader:

> The houses don't like the dust that gnaws in the corners and spills over the evening windows that no one bothers to clean. It was better before the dust. It was better when we had rain coming through the

roofs. Soaked or not we stood our ground . . . Yes, we heard the shooting. We were threatened too. We had stones through our windows and fire ripping through our bowels, but we still stood, even though we were empty. Had we not seen many twists of fate? . . . Forever coming and going, that is the way with people—they are restless things compared to us houses. We remember them though, the ones that built us even though they are gone . . . Before long there will be nothing left but stones, gravestones along the valley, sinking back into the earth from whence we came. But even then we will not forget because our memory is in the stone and our stone knows the touch of red hands that lifted us and pushed us slowly into place. It was not earthquake or flood that despoiled us but a fountain pen and soft fingers . . . Foreign voices scrape the pale blue sky. Measuring, surveying, deciding . . . Men in yellow hats peering at grey papers. Restless insects crawling in the cemetries of giants. What right have you? It was not your forefathers who built us . . . But we will not forget. Our memory is in our stone; the touch of red hands is still upon our skin; your soft hands will not scrub it clean . . .

If that's not bitter passion and commitment, I don't know what is.

All the same there is a danger that in other post-modern writers a would-be sophisticated cynicism could rob their work of its humanity. John Rowlands, while obviously irritated by those who scorn post-modernism, does issue a warning. 'There's a loss of innocence now,' he says. 'We tend to speak in a kind of parody. We're unable to say anything without wearing a perpetual, ironical smile. For it is wiser to smile than to cry.'

This new perception could be seen in an interesting discussion published in *Taliesin* between writer David Lodge and Ioan Williams. David Lodge suggested that post-modernism started with a desire to break new ground, that there was a feeling that everything had already been done and that the new way was through a kind of parodying, ironic self-orientation. One feels, he said, that by now a cul-de-sac has been reached in the way this game can be played; that its whole purpose in the first place was to create shock but that now it's become a kind of convention and is losing its effect.

I hope David Lodge is right. After all, books need readers. Writers don't work in a vacuum, and we can't live in an ivory tower for long. We want our books to be bought, read and give pleasure. In the meantime *Tu Chwith* (currently under the joint editorship of Angharad Price and Sioned Puw Rowlands) stimulates, shocks, irritates, puzzles, but is like a breath of fresh air. No, more like a fresh gale on the literary scene. I hope it has a long life.

And now a brief look at drama, both in the theatre and on radio and television. Radio in English has given us an occasional series of plays reflecting the exciting stirrings in Welsh theatre in recent years. At one time it looked as though the arts in Radio Cymru were going to be down-graded, but now comes a new drama series, 'Chwaraeddy Comedi', which looks promising. On television, the magazine 'Slate' packs in a lot and has had some memorable items, but its rather breathless presentation and idiosyncratic camera work leaves this viewer, for one, rather exhausted. In Welsh television there are, as ever, minuses and pluses. Gwyn Thomas, who in the past, was responsible for some of the most innovative television plays in verse, is particularly criticial of the absence of poetry on both radio and television. Perhaps 'they' think that the ever-popular 'Talwrn y Beirdd', the bardic competition with competing teams is going to satisfy that need, though one has the feeling that most people listen to 'Talwrn' mainly for the laughs and the witty comments of the adjudicator, Gerallt Lloyd Owen— nothing wrong with that, of course, and, indeed, where else would you find a popular game contest between poets with a very diversified audience lapping it up? But there is an increasing feeling that both radio and television in Welsh are fighting shy of serious arts programmes, possibly because they've decided to concentrate on young viewers and listeners with a limited concentration span.

Gerwyn Wiliams's crown-winning poem 'Dolenni' at the 1994 National Eisteddfod, was a warning against the new parochialism in television. Soaps have become more real than life for too many people, he implied, and there was this compulsion to make even news programmes into entertainment.

But there are bright spots. An international audience was made aware of Alan Llwyd's film, *Hedd Wyn* (directed by Paul

Turner), when it was Oscar-nominated for the best foreign language film in 1994, and there are others like Endaf Emlyn's beautifully-shot film, *Y Mapiwr*, and Gareth Lloyd Williams's *Y Wisg Sidan* and, indeed, many others. There has been critical acclaim for a number of plays in English from BBC Wales, a series of low-budget half-hour single dramas, sadly not shown on the network. Karl Francis, the recent Head of BBC Drama in Wales had become increasingly concerned about this. For some reason or other, he says, there is a reluctance on the part of London to network plays about Wales or Welsh characters. If the occasional character does appear in London plays, he is usually the stereotyped 'Twp Taffy'. In a recent *Western Mail* article, an exasperated Karl Francis wrote, 'It's easier to cast an ethnic or disabled actor than a Welsh one.' And it seems to me that the only time Wales gets a mention in London papers is when it carries the prefix 'Princess of . . .'

In Welsh-language theatre we have a number of original writers—Siôn Eirian, Gareth Miles, Twm Miall, Geraint Lewis, and, in particular, Meic Povey, who seems, of all, to have inherited Gwenlyn Parry's mantle, for his well-constructed, thought-provoking and utterly convincing plays. In fact, one can only skim over the theatrical scene in Wales. What is happening needs a whole talk devoted to it. The works of these young dramatists have been given an impetus by the number of small, brave companies that have arisen in the last 20 years or so, companies like Bara Caws, Brith Gof, Dalier Sylw, and so on.

No, we have no National Theatre, though the call for it has been re-awakened during the last year, particularly by Michael Bogdanov, the well-known director. But other voices are cautious, some suggesting that while we have these small drama companies, working in different parts of Wales, we have no need for a National Theatre concentrated on one place, and David Adams, Arts correspondent to *The Guardian* suggests that such a move would be completely contrary to the unique way theatre has developed in Wales.

Now, you may be wondering what it is that Welsh writers write about? What triggers off that urge to fill a blank sheet of paper? Because, even if you delight in not being a 'realistic' writer, you must have some starting point, some vital urge to communicate, which, in the case of a novelist, for instance, makes you willing to sacrifice not hours, but perhaps years of your life to your creation.

For those like Angharad Tomos, there's no problem. I once heard her say that writers in Wales should, above all, devote themselves to writing about the language struggle. She herself has certainly done more than just write about the language struggle, but I feel there is a danger here for less able writers, a danger that overt propaganda, however sincere, can destroy the best-intentioned of works and do more harm than good.

Poetry, by its very nature, is less oblique, more personal than prose. For writers like R.S. Thomas, Gillian Clarke, Gerallt Lloyd Owen, Iwan Llwyd, Myrddin ap Dafydd, Nesta Wyn Jones and Emyr Lewis—there is a gnawing awareness of the danger to our very existence.

In a recent article in *Golwg*, Emyr Humphreys says that a perception of crisis is what animates most present-day literature, especially in drama and the novel. And perhaps it's a cliché for me to add that this crisis in Wales is one of identity. In order to remind ourselves of our identity we delve into our ancient history and legends. It is not surprising that so many have wrenched inspiration from the *Mabinogion*. In an article in the book *Diffinio Dwy Lenyddiaeth Cymru*, Jane Aaron writes about the influence of the story of Blodeuwedd on women writers in both languages. Blodeuwedd, you may remember, was the woman created from flowers, but created without any moral sense. Because of her adultery with Gronw Pebr, she is turned into an owl. Gillian Clarke describes her punishment thus:

> Deprived too of afternoons
> in the comfortable sisterhood
> of women moving in kitchens
> among cups, cloths, and running
> water while they talk.

(Gillian Clarke is particularly good at evoking domestic life. Then follows a picture of Blodeuwedd as a scapegoat for the wrongs of her sisters.)

200

Her night lament,
beyond conversation,
the owl follows
her shadow like a cross
over the fields.

Blodeuwedd's ballad
where the long reach
of the peninsula
is black in a sea
aghast with gazing.

Angharad Jones, who has recently been made Script Commissioner for S4C, has not only used this theme in her medal winning novel, *Y Dylluan Wen* (The White Owl), but is another who has written several poems on the theme of Blodeuwedd.

It is interesting that, in her article, Jane Aaron perceived a difference between the more liberated attitude to sexual desire in women who write in English and the way Welsh women writers are wracked by the destructive results of illicit sex. One explanation could be in the movement of families away from their rural roots in this century. I suppose it's right to say that more Welsh novels now have an urban setting rather than a rural one. This is inevitable when the ambitious young flock to the towns and cities, where a new city-orientated culture has arisen in Wales. I think it began with Siôn Eirian's *Bob yn y Ddinas*, a novel which showed for the first time the seamy side of Cardiff life amid Welsh drop-outs. Manon Rhys's *Cysgodion* describes people in a university town grappling with domestic problems in the new moral ethos of the times. This novel bears out Jane Aaron's contention. Lois Daniel's friend has warned her that her illicit love-affair would destroy her in the end, and Manon Rhys pulls no punches in describing her heroine's nemesis.

In Welsh we have a saying *bwrw swildod*, which means shedding shyness, usually applied to newly-weds on honeymoon. Today's writers have certainly done their *bwrw swildod*, even though, perhaps, the rather too prolific use of the 'F' word does remind one of a child who has just learnt to say a naughty

201

word. A far cry from Kate Roberts and Islwyn Ffowc Elis. But both *Bob yn y Ddinas* and *Cysgodion* are brave novels. I particularly liked the skilful way Manon Rhys tells the story of a woman researching the life of artist Gwen John by weaving it in counterpoint with her own turbulent life.

There's so much more to be said. What about our internationally known poet, R.S. Thomas, you'll be wondering. It's like discussing Irish literature without mentioning Seamus Heaney. Or Emyr Humphreys, whose latest novel *Unconditional Surrender*, was published in 1996. What about John Davies's magisterial, *The History of Wales*, one of the most important volumes of the century? What about the growth of pop and rock culture and the lyrics that have reflected the language struggle and the longings and hopes of young people? And what about Tŷ Newydd at Llanystumdwy where budding writers can try out their skills under the watchful eyes of old hands? They are all important. Wales is entering a period of profound change, technological as well as political, and there's no doubt that it will all galvanise new creative energy here. Already there's a lot of discussion going on, a lot of argument, a lot of puzzlement, and every year the Literature Pavilion at the National Eisteddfod provides a stimulating platform on which we can air our grievances and our hopes, to say nothing of our quarrels—all important for our creative health.

Certainly we are on the verge of an exciting new chapter in Welsh literature. I'm sure that our experience here in Wales has similarities with those of the other five Celtic nations. What is important is that we can look outward and gain inspiration and support from each other.